THE COMPLETE HANDBOOK OF

HEALTH TIPS

Based on the latest
Dietary and Scientific Findings
and Traditional Remedies

By
R. Emil Neuman

Designed and typeset by SJ Design and Publishing

Printed by Repro City Ltd London

ISBN 1 85779 079 0

Introduction

This book contains a treasury of health information drawn from the latest medical and nutritional literature and time-proven remedies.

This book is arranged by subject matter. Each topic is covered in a clear, concise manner. You can quickly scan through the book and focus on the topics of particular interest to you. However, I urge you to read the entire book. It gives a wealth of interesting and valuable health information of vital importance to you and your family.

While the book should prove to be an extremely valuable source of health information, an important caution should be understood: this book is not intended to be a substitute for medical advice from a doctor. Don't attempt to self-diagnose a medical condition or embark on self-treatment of a serious ailment. This can be dangerous. Seek the best medical treatment when needed.

Please enjoy the book and I wish you the very best.

ACNE

Avoid Acne Flareups. Acne is caused by clogging and inflammation of the oil glands and ducts beneath the skin. This causes the acne pimples and blackheads. About 75% of adolescent boys and 50% of adolescent girls develop acne. The following can cause acne flareups:

- *Cosmetics.* Acne flareups can be due to use of cleansing creams, night moisturisers, face foundations and blushers. These products often contain additives such as fatty acids, coal tars and oils that clog pores.
- *Foods.* Foods and vitamin supplements containing iodine may aggravate acne, says Dr James Fulton, of the Acne Research Institute, Newport Beach, California.
- *Poor Hygiene.* When dirt and oil build up it can clog pores and cause a flareup.

Home Care Suggestions.
- For mild to moderate cases of acne, benzoyl peroxide is recommended. Benzoyl peroxide is available at most chemists. It unclogs skin pores and promotes new skin growth. Rubbing ice cubes on the face for three minutes before applying medication helps, according to Dr James Fulton of the Acne Research Centre in California. Ice reduces inflammation. Wrap ice in a face cloth to avoid freezing your hand.
- The traditional treatment for acne has been the antibiotic tetracycline. However, a Swedish study showed zinc to be as effective as tetracycline without the side effects. A study performed in Sweden gave 19 acne patients 135 mg of zinc a day and a second group of 18, 750 mg a day of tetracycline. After 12 weeks both groups showed a 67% improvement in their complexion. It is believed that zinc works to clear acne by reducing irritation and inflammation and by helping the damaged skin heal itself. Consult your doctor before taking zinc supplements.
- Research has shown that a low zinc diet can bring on acne flareups in 10 to 14 days. Be sure your diet provides adequate amounts of zinc. Foods rich in zinc include seafood, spinach, mushrooms, whole grain rice and sunflower seeds.

• Many people have reported that applying vitamin A from capsules helps soothe acne.

AGE SPOTS

Try Taking Zinc. Age spots are those dark, purple blemish marks on the skin of older people caused by the haemorrhaging of tiny blood vessels under the skin.

A study conducted at England's East Birmingham Hospital revealed that elderly people with age spots had a low level of zinc in their bodies. When zinc levels were increased, the age spots disappeared. Foods rich in zinc include seafood, onions, soya beans, spinach and whole grains.

AIDS

Some Facts You Should Know. Many people worry that they may catch AIDS other than through sexual contact. But it is not possible to catch the disease, for example, from food prepared by someone with AIDS or from plates they have touched.

Another common worry concerns the danger of infection from mosquitoes. However, there have been no known cases of AIDS being spread by mosquito or other insect bites.

Whilst you can't catch AIDS through a kiss on the cheek, there is a danger from romantic kissing because the virus has been found in saliva. Despite this, there are no known cases of AIDS being passed on in this way.

A question often asked is whether people can be immune to the AIDS virus. Research has shown that some people may be immune, and scientists are studying them to see if their body makeup can help them in producing a vaccine against AIDS.

AIR TRAVEL

Reducing Pressure In Ears. Many people experience extreme discomfort while flying in an aeroplane. This pain is caused by air pressure in the cabin creating a vacuum in the middle ear. The pain can get very severe unless something is done to balance the air pressure in the middle ear.

What To Do To Avoid Discomfort. Many people get relief by chewing gum or sucking on mints. Swallowing air while chewing the gum tends to balance the pressure in the middle ear.

- When chewing gum does not work, many people get relief by closing their mouths, pinching their nose shut and gently blowing out their cheeks. If a clicking noise is heard this means the procedure has been successful.
- If these measures do not result in relief straight away keep on trying them.

ALCOHOLISM (See also HANGOVERS)

Tips For Minimising Alcohol Effects. Heavy alcohol use can cause hepatitis, cirrhosis of the liver, gastritis (a painful inflammation of the stomach lining), neuritis (inflammation of the nerves) and vitamin deficiencies.

Heavy drinking may be worse than cigarettes in contributing to oral cancer. Researchers say that people who smoke 40 cigarettes a day stand a five times greater risk of getting oral cancer than non-smokers. But people who drink 6 ounces of whisky a day run a 15.2 times greater risk of getting oral cancer than non-smokers, according to Dr Arthur Mashburg and Dr Lawrence Garfinkel. Here are some suggestions for minimising the harmful effects of alcohol:

- Drinking alcohol depletes the body of vitamins, especially vitamin B, says Dr Boras Tabakoff, Director of the Alcoholism and Drug Abuse Research and Training Programme at the University of Illinois Medical Centre. When drinking, take a Vitamin B-complex.
- To help prevent a hangover from alcohol consumption take one 50 mg B-complex tablet before going out. Also take one while you're drinking. This will help replace the B vitamins that alcohol destroys in your body.
- Excessive alcohol can spark a zinc deficiency by flushing stored zinc out of the liver. Insufficient zinc can cause prostate troubles and problems with sex, says Dr Carl Pfeiffer, from the Bio-Brain Centre, Princeton, New Jersey. Supplement your diet with zinc when drinking heavily.
- Other nutrients destroyed by alcohol are magnesium, vitamin A, C, D and calcium. Just two or three drinks per day will start to deplete these nutrients. It's a good idea to take a multi-vitamin daily when drinking heavily.

ALLERGIES

How To Live With An Allergy. An allergy is a reaction or sensitivity to a substance in the environment called an allergen. Common symptoms of allergy are watery eyes, runny nose, itchy and inflamed skin. Other symptoms are headaches and sinus stuffiness.

We get allergic reactions from breathing air containing allergens, touching things with allergens and eating foods containing allergens.

Identifying the specific allergens that cause reactions may be time-consuming, painful and expensive. Often specific allergens are never discovered.

Avoiding Allergens In The Air. Allergies can be avoided by minimising exposure to common allergens in the air. Here are some tips:

- On windy days during the pollen season do not play golf, hike, go horse riding or jogging.
- Minimise early morning outdoor activity. Pollen generally is emitted from sunrise to 10am. If you drive to work during those hours keep your windows closed.
- Don't install a window fan. It will exhaust house air and bring in allergens through open windows. Instead, install a central or window air-conditioner unit which will recirculate air in the rooms where windows are shut.
- Dust daily with chemically treated or oil dust cloth so you won't spread the dust around.
- Vacuum carpets and rugs daily changing the vacuum bags frequently.
- Keep pets away from the general living area. Never let them sleep in the bedroom, especially on your bed.
- A cat's litter box is a prime source of allergens.
- Enclose your pillow and mattress in plastic. This will reduce dust and mites that can trigger an allergic reaction.
- Keep your bedroom free of objects that collect dust. This would include magazines, books, cuddle toys and ornaments. Dust and vacuum frequently.
- Keep house plants out of your home. They can trigger an allergic reaction from moulds that form on them when they are wet.

- Try using an artificial Christmas tree. Live trees contain hydrocarbons that can carry moulds and be irritating.
- Keep your grass trimmed short. No taller than one inch. This reduces exposure to grass pollen.
- Do not use aerosol sprays.
- If your home has a forced air heating system try putting a cheese cloth over the vent. This will act as a filter and catch most of the dust.
- If possible get an air-conditioner unit for your home.

Testing For Allergens In Things. To determine whether you may be allergic to some kind of fabric or material, place a small piece of it in a jar and put the jar in the sun or a warm place for several hours. Then remove the lid and smell the air in the jar. Keep track of any reactions you may experience. If you have no symptoms, you are probably not allergic to that item in the jar.

Identifying Food Allergies. Millions of people are allergic to certain foods and don't know it. But there is a simple test you can do to identify allergen foods, say Dr Arthur F Coca, allergist and immunologist. Dr Coca recommends taking your pulse before and after meals. For example, let's say you suspect that you may be allergic to oranges. One morning, take your pulse when you get up. Then eat an orange. Wait 30 to 60 minutes, then take your pulse again. See if there's any abnormal increase in your pulse rate. While this test is not 100% accurate, in a large number of cases an increase in pulse rate indicates an allergy to a food or substance. To take your pulse, lightly press two or three fingers on your wrist. Do not use your thumb because your thumb has a pulse of its own.

Foods most commonly causing allergies: corn, eggs, fish, milk, nuts, wheat. Foods that often cause allergies: alcohol, berries, buckwheat, cane sugar, chocolate, coconut, coffee, mustard, oranges and citrus fruits, peanut butter, peas, pork, potatoes, soya, tomatoes, yeast.

Look Out For Fruits And Vegetables. Pesticides and preservatives on fruits and vegetables can be a prime source of allergens. To remove pesticides, soak the fruit or vegetables in a sink filled with water and a quarter cup of vinegar. Then scrub the fruits and vegetables and rinse them under cold water.

Grain Allergens. Grains are a major allergen source. It's a good idea to transfer grain products including rice, flour and cereals into glass or metal containers. This will prevent mould and insect infestation that can cause allergies. Keep the containers in a cool, dry place.

ALZHEIMER'S DISEASE

Research Studies To Consider. This is a disorder in elderly persons caused by a degeneration of the blood vessels of the brain, resulting in brain shrinkage. There is a steady decline in brain function, memory and personality. Victims often cannot recognise family members and close friends. Alzheimer's disease affects about 10% of persons over age 65. There is no known treatment.

- A preliminary Dutch study evaluated patients with Alzheimer's type senility and alcohol-related brain damage and found low levels of vitamin B-12 and zinc in both groups. Researchers believe that early recognition and adequate treatment with B-12 and zinc can possibly prevent irreversible damage to patients with these disorders. This study was published in the Journal of Orthomolecular Psychiatry.
- In a preliminary research study ten patients with Alzheimer's disease were given choline in their diets. The average age of the patients was 77. Three of the ten patients seemed less confused after the choline treatment.

    Researchers believe choline may work best before the onset of Alzheimer's disease. When choline was given to patients under 65 in the early stages of the disease all patients reported improvement in memory. Lecithin is rich in choline. Lecithin is available at most health food stores. This study was reported in the medical journal Lancet.

ANAL ITCHING

How To Avoid Anal Itching. Common causes of this condition include intestinal pinworms, haemorrhoids, allergies and eating highly spicy foods. Coffee, tea, colas and chocolate may irritate bowels and cause anal itching, says Dr Lester Tavel of Pearland, Texas. Most sufferers have excess mucus that seeps through the anal canal keeping the area moist and irritated. Tips to avoid anal itching:

- Keep the anal area dry and clean. Use of oily medications only worsen the condition.
- A dusting powder should be used daily. This is preferable to an anti-fungal preparation.
- Avoid beverages and foods that contain caffeine.

Yoghurt For Itching - A Study To Consider. A preliminary study published in "Diseases of the Colon and Rectum" showed people suffering from anal itching were helped by lactobacillus acidophilus. Of the 87 people participating in the study, 74 said that itching completely disappeared or substantially subsided. Researchers recommend adding acidophilus obtained from yoghurt to your diet. Both lactobacillus acidophilus and orlactobacillus bulgaricus are contained in yoghurt. Either will provide the same benefits.

ANGINA

Cause Of Pain. Angina is a pain in the chest caused by a lack of oxygen in the heart. This lack of oxygen is normally caused by a narrowing of the arteries due to cholesterol formation. The pain may feel like indigestion and it may shoot to the arm. Angina occurs whenever the heart requires more oxygen than the narrowed arteries can provide.

Things To Avoid.
- Don't engage in sudden, strenuous physical activity. Always warm up first.
- Don't overeat. Eat at regular intervals.
- Rest for 30 minutes after meals, especially heavy meals.
- Sleep in a well-ventilated room.
- Try to avoid constipation.
- See your doctor for regular checkups.

Preliminary Research To Consider.

- *Vitamin E.* According to Dr Terence W Anderson of the University of British Columbia, vitamin E may help angina discomfort. Dr Anderson conducted a study of 15 angina patients who were already taking vitamin E. Without the patients knowing, seven were given fake pills containing no vitamin E. After three weeks three patients had to drop out of the study because of severe angina pain. A fourth stayed on but complained of increased pain. The remaining eight who continued taking vitamin E daily had no increase in the angina pain. Foods rich in vitamin E include dark green vegetables, fruits and rice.

- *Lecithin/Vitamin E.* Researchers reported treating angina with 800 mg and more of vitamin E a day. Favourable responses have been reported with lecithin using 15 g a day.

- *Aspirin.* Based on a study of 11,965 men having heart conditions, the Federal Food and Drug Administration concluded that it is safe and effective to take one aspirin a day to control angina. Among men suffering unstable angina who took an aspirin each day, the risk of dying from heart attack dropped about one-half.

  One regular 325 mg aspirin should be the daily dose. Of course, you should continue to see your doctor at regular intervals. Aspirin appears to help prevent clotting of the blood which can cause heart attack. The Food and Drug Administration emphasised that aspirin therapy is not a substitute for other preventative measures such as stopping smoking, eating better, losing weight and taking sensible exercise.

- *Amino Acid-L-Carnitive.* Preliminary studies done by Dr Robert Atkins show that this amino acid may be valuable in relieving the pain of angina.

- *Tilting Bed.* Many people suffer angina attacks at night. Tilting the head of the bed upward 10 degrees may reduce angina pain. Lying flat increases the amount of blood returning to the heart, reducing oxygen flow. The best way to tilt a bed is to put wooden blocks under front legs.

ANOREXIA NERVOSA

Crucial Anorexia Fact. This is an eating disorder that strikes younger women who suppress the urge to eat to the point of malnutrition and even starvation.

- 95% of sufferers are female, mostly in their teens.
- It mostly strikes obedient girls who try too hard to please parents, teachers and others. This creates a subconscious need to control at least one part of their lives - eating.
- Victims often fear growing up so they unconsciously "diet away" physical signs of maturity - curved hips, larger breasts etc.
- Anorexia sufferers need professional counselling.

Zinc - Preliminary Research. One preliminary study showed that supplements of the mineral zinc were 80% successful in helping sufferers overcome anorexia, says Dr Douglas Latto, British Nutrition Foundation in London. Zinc supplements helped patients regain appetite and put on weight.

When the anorexia victim stops eating the body begins to lose zinc. As the zinc levels in the body go down the sense of taste and smell is destroyed. Without these senses the desire for food declines even further. But when anorexics were given zinc they regained these senses. Their appetites returned and they started eating again. Zinc supplements of more than 50 mg per day are not recommended without medical supervision. Foods rich in zinc include seafood, spinach, mushrooms, whole grains and sunflower seeds.

ANTIBIOTICS

Kill Both Bad And Good Bacteria. Antibiotics kill the good bacteria in your body as well as the harmful bacteria. Killing off beneficial bacteria can cause diarrhoea and other stomach problems. When the beneficial bacteria is destroyed it can cause fungus to grow in the intestines, vagina, lungs and mouth.

When taking antibiotics be sure to take generous amounts of acidophilus culture to help maintain the beneficial bacteria in your body. Acidophilus culture can be obtained through eating yoghurt or taking acidophilus capsules. Both are available at most health food shops.

ANTS

Stopping Ant Attacks. Ants may carry germs that can cause disease. To stop ants from crawling into your home through cracks in the walls try putting a little petroleum jelly in the cracks. Also sprinkle red pepper around your kitchen work surfaces. Ants can't stand red pepper. Plant mint near your front and back door. Ants do not like mint.

ARTHRITIS

Fish Oil. Taking fish oil capsules may relieve the symptoms of rheumatoid arthritis even when conventional treatment doesn't, according to an Australian study published in the Journal of Rheumatology. Over three months, subjects showed a reduction in joint soreness and an improvement in grip strength. But they were taking a high dosage (18 g per day) and as the long-term effects of this may be harmful, such a treatment should only be taken under medical supervision.

Vitamin C. Preliminary British research shows that the correction of vitamin C deficiency in rheumatoid arthritis sufferers may greatly reduce the bruising which is one of the symptoms of the disease. However, there is no evidence that extra doses of vitamin C will help someone who is not lacking the vitamin.

ASPIRIN

Suggestions To Avoid Stomach Upset.
- Aspirin will cause less digestive upset if taken after eating food and with a full glass of water.
- Avoid combining aspirin with acidic foods such as citrus fruits and juices, alcoholic drinks. They may increase irritation in the stomach.
- Never take aspirin with vitamin C. This will increase possibility of stomach bleeding.
- Aspirin with an enteric coating reduces irritation to the stomach. The enteric coating delays absorption of aspirin until it reaches the intestine.

ASTHMA

Things That Trigger An Attack. This condition is caused by an obstruction of the bronchial tubes brought about by a sensitivity to substances in the environment and other factors.

According to the American Lung Association the most common things that can trigger an asthma attack are:

- Household products such as paint thinner and chlorine bleach.
- Cold and extra humid air.
- Air pollution.
- Exercise.
- Infections caused by colds and viruses.
- Tobacco smoke.
- Emotions such as anger, fear and even happiness.
- Pollen, mould and spores; hair and feathers, and certain foods such as chocolate, nuts and eggs.

Tips On Preventing Attacks.
- Avoid food that contains preservatives and dyes.
- Avoid aspirin.
- Avoid cola drinks.
- Avoid cold liquids. Cold liquids may shock your bronchial tubes into asthma spasm.
- Keep the air clean in your home. Use air filters to trap dust and mould particles.
- Avoid dogs and cats including short-haired breeds. Dogs and cats give off dander - tiny particles from the hair and skin that can produce reactions.
- Avoid feathered pillows.
- Choose the right kind of carpeting. The backing of many carpets is made of jute, which may induce allergic reactions. Choose foam-rubber backing and padding instead.
- Do not wallpaper bedrooms. Mould can grow behind the paper.
- Buy synthetic Christmas trees. Real trees contain mould.
- Keep windows closed when air pollution is high outside.

• Wear a scarf over your mouth in cold weather, but avoid woollen scarves which may trigger an allergic reaction.

Mushrooms Can Trigger An Attack. Mushroom spores are released into the open air after mushrooms ripen and have been harvested. If you like mushrooms get the tinned ones that are packed in liquid. Most mushrooms release spores once a year in the autumn. Cultivated mushrooms release spores all the year round.

Stay Away From Salad Bars. Many items in a salad bar are treated with bisulphates. These are food preservatives that keep food looking fresh while out in the open for hours at a time. They can cause serious adverse reactions in persons having asthma. The Food and Drug Administration is aware of about 90 deaths from adverse reactions to these preservatives.

Getting Relief - Research To Consider.
• *Coffee.* A few cups of coffee may relieve asthma symptoms, according to studies conducted at the University of Manitoba in Winnepeg, Canada. Researchers found that the caffeine equivalent to two cups of coffee unclogged blocked bronchial passages in the lungs. This study was reported in the New England Journal of Medicine.
• *Vitamin C.* Taking vitamin C may help control asthma attacks. In one study researchers gave asthmatics 1,000 mg of vitamin C a day. Those taking vitamin C had about 25% fewer attacks than those who received a fake pill. When the subjects stopped taking vitamin C, they once again suffered the same number of asthma episodes as the people who did not take the vitamin C. This study was published in the Journal of Tropical and Geographical Medicine. Foods rich in vitamin C include citrus fruits and fruit juices, berries, cabbage, green vegetables and potatoes.
• *Vitamin B-6.* In a study of 15 asthmatics given 50 mg of vitamin B-6 twice daily, symptoms were relieved in every case, says Dr Robert Reynolds, a US Department of Agriculture research chemist. Foods rich in vitamin B-6 include bananas, cabbage, green leafy vegetables, whole grains and fish.

Deep Breathing Exercise For Relief. According to the American Lung Association, breathing correctly can relieve wheezing, chest tightness and shortness of breath. The following exercise can be practised lying down, sitting or standing. It should be done daily for maximum benefit.

1. Think of your chest and stomach as a container for air. Breathe in through your nose slowly filling the bottom of the container first. Continue until the stomach feels inflated like a balloon. If you place your hand on the spot just above your naval you can feel your middle rise and fall with each breath. Exhale slowly through your mouth. The container should feel completely empty and your stomach should feel flat before you inhale again.
2. Repeat. Inhale and exhale 12 times.

Relaxing Away An Asthma Attack. The American Lung Association teaches children to relax as a way of warding off an asthma attack. The following exercise when practised for five minutes a day can be used whenever the chest starts to feel tight or other signs occur. This exercise works for adults also.

- Stand up and make all your muscles very tight. Then take a deep breath. Point your chin up to the ceiling and grit your teeth. Hold your arms out straight. Keep your elbows tight and your fists tightly closed. Your legs and toes should be stiff. Hold for a few seconds.
- Then let everything go like a balloon that's been deflated. Completely relax all your muscles until you feel like a wet rag or noodle.
- Flop to the floor in a lying position and stay there. Close your eyes. Keep your arms limp and loose. Your face and feet should be limp also.
- Picture yourself floating down a river. Concentrate on each muscle and how nice and floppy it feels.
- Breathe softly and easily as if you were fast asleep in your bed. Stay quiet and relaxed and feel how pleasant it is.
- Open your eyes. Turn on the relaxed wet rag feeling whenever you feel nervous or short of breath, or feel an asthma attack coming on.

ATHLETE'S FOOT

4 Suggestions For Preventing. Athlete's foot is a fungus infection between the toes and on the balls of the feet. It causes itching, burning and stinging. The skin becomes red and cracks.

Whenever the space between the toes remains moist the fungus can take hold. The fungus can be caught quickly by walking barefoot in a gym or locker room. To avoid problems:

- Wear protective footwear to avoid contact with the floor.
- Dry feet thoroughly with a clean towel - especially between the toes.
- Change socks every day - twice a day in extremely hot weather.
- Use dusting powder to keep feet dry.

Home Care Of Athlete's Foot.
- Bathe feet several times a day with soap and warm water. Dry feet and sprinkle with athlete's foot powder, available at chemists.
- Several types of athlete's foot preparations are available at chemists. Directions usually call for morning and night applications until symptoms go away.
- At night separate toes with cotton balls to reduce friction on inflamed skin.
- Wear open toe shoes in hot weather.

BACK GARDEN BARBECUES

Safety Tips To Follow. An outside barbecue in the back garden can be dangerous, especially with children. The heat intensity from the fire can reach up to 500 degrees. This temperature is the same inside or outside the grill. The following suggestions will help avoid an accident:

- Keep the grill at least 6 ft away from the house.
- Water the ground around the grill lightly before lighting the coals.
- When using lighter fluid, first soak the coals. Then wait 5 or 10 minutes before striking a match.
- Never add more lighter fluid after the fire is blazing.

- Once fire is lit stay in the area to make sure the fire stays under control and children stay away from the grill.
- Wait until the coals are glowing evenly before starting to cook.

BACK PAIN

17 Simple Tips To Help Prevent Back Trouble.

- Don't stand or sit in one position for a long period of time while working.
- While on the telephone avoid holding the telephone between your ear and neck for long periods of time. This can tense the muscles in your shoulder and cause back trouble.
- While driving long distances in your car, stop periodically and take a break. After you've been driving for a while, don't make any sudden movements that could pull a muscle.
- Sleep on a firm mattress. The harder the mattress, the better.
- Use pillows with manufactured fibres. Foam rubber pillows tend to elevate your head higher than it should be, thus crimping your neck.
- Wear comfortable shoes. The higher the heel, the greater the risk of back pain.
- When carrying anything on your shoulder switch the weight to the other shoulder from time to time.
- When lifting, keep your back straight and bend your knees. Let your leg muscles do most of the work. Hold the object you're trying to lift close to your body.
- Never stretch when you're reaching for a high object.
- Don't bend over furniture to open or close windows.
- Always push a large object, never pull it. Pulling places a great strain on the muscles of the lower back.
- While sitting down, keep your knees about an inch higher than your hips. This reduces the strain on your lower and upper back muscles.
- Before doing work spend a few minutes warming up. Warming up exercises should include bending, stretching and twisting.
- When going to bed lie on your side and draw one or both knees up towards your chin. This is a good resting position for your back.

- If you sleep on your stomach, put a pillow under your abdomen so your back is raised slightly. The worst sleeping position for your back is flat on your stomach with your head raised on a pillow.
- When getting out of bed in the morning be careful.
- After sitting or standing in one position for more than 10 minutes, avoid any sudden or forced movement. For example, be careful when you're watching television and the phone rings or when you're in your car and you get out quickly.

BAD BREATH (HALITOSIS)

7 Tips To Avoid Bad Breath. Bad breath may be caused by poor mouth hygiene, throat infection, teeth and gum decay, excessive smoking or the presence of bacteria in the mouth. The following suggestions may help avoid bad breath:

- *Acidophilus.* Bad breath is often associated with putrefactive bacteria living on undigested food in the stomach. This condition causes gas to be released through the breath. Supplementing the diet with the friendly bacteria lactobacillus acidophilus often helps. Acidophilus can be obtained from yoghurt or in capsule or milk form - available at most health food shops.
- *Brushing Your Tongue.* Dr Joseph Toncetich from the School of Dentistry, University of British Columbia in Vancouver, Canada, performed a study to find out the best way to reduce bad breath. Eight volunteers, all of whom suffered from morning bad breath, participated in the study. The doctor found that brushing teeth reduced mouth odour by about 25%. Brushing the teeth and the tongue reduced mouth odour by 85%. This study was published in the journal called Oral Surgery.
- *Mouth Washes.* Most contain high concentrations of alcohol. The alcohol kills bacteria in the mouth but only temporarily. When the bacteria return, more come back than before you used the mouth wash. Many dentists believe the alcohol-laced mouth wash can damage the tissue in the mouth, cause inflammation and result in bad breath.
- *Avoid Garlic, Onions, Fish And Alcohol.* They contain compounds that produce excessive odour when dissolved in the mouth.

- *Eat Parsley.* It contains chlorophyll which absorbs mouth odours when chewed.
- *Go for Citrus as well as Mint Flavours.* Citrus flavoured drinks and sweets stimulate salivation and activate the mouth's self-cleaning process.
- *Try Baking Soda and Hydrogen Peroxide.* According to Dr Dan Watt, DDS, of the International Dental Health Foundation, a good way to freshen bad breath is to brush once a day (preferably before bed) with a home-made toothpaste made of one teaspoonful of baking soda and a capful of hydrogen peroxide. The baking soda is an abrasive which removes the bacteria and also kills it, while the hydrogen peroxide produces oxygen bubbles which also destroy the germs.

BALDNESS

New Drug Offers Hope. Researchers at the San Antonio, Texas, Health Science Centre say a new drug called Minoxidil actually stimulates hair growth on scalps of bald men. Nearly half of 619 people testing Minoxidil experienced moderate to heavy hair growth.

Minoxidil was originally used for controlling high blood pressure. Doctors became interested when patients reported hair growth as a result of using the medicine. Studies have shown the compound is safe with no side effects, but it has yet to be approved by the Food and Drug Administration.

BEAUTY TIPS

Emergency Beauty Tips. If you're running late and feel a mess, here's how to brighten yourself up ... in less than 10 minutes.
- *Greasy Hair.* Talcum powder will absorb the grease. Sprinkle in a tablespoonful, rub it gently through your hair, then leave it on for three minutes. Lean forward and brush it out.
- *A Spot on your Face.* Wrap an ice cube in a handkerchief and press it on the spot for three seconds. Take it off for three seconds then repeat the procedure twice. The spot will shrink and disappear temporarily.
- *Saggy Facial Skin.* Give yourself an instant facial - cover your face, avoiding the eye area, with Pepto-Bismol. Let it dry and rinse off with cool water.

- *Stains*. If you've spilt food on your blouse and there's no time to soak it, immediately apply club soda and rub with a clean, dry cloth, repeating if necessary.

BEDSORES

4 Tips For Avoiding Bedsores.
- Vitamin C. The healing rate of bedsores can be improved by taking up to 500 mg of vitamin C a day.
- Use of inflated rubber cushions helps avoid bedsores.
- Shifting body with pillows helps prevent sores.
- Keep bed clothing loose.

BETA-CAROTENE

May Lower Cancer Risk. Most of the latest research on cancer focuses on vitamin A in the form of beta-carotene. Research shows low levels of beta-carotene increase risk of lung cancer and other cancers. Beta-carotene is amply found in carrots, dark leafy greens, sweet potatoes and other vegetables. Once inside your body, beta-carotene is converted into vitamin A. In getting daily sources of vitamin A, it is better to use beta-carotene supplements than plain vitamin A.

BIO-FLAVONOIDS

Helps Vitamin C Absorption. These are compounds found in the white pulp of oranges, grapefruits and other citrus fruits and vegetables. Bio-flavonoids enhance the body's absorption of vitamin C. Studies show that citrus bio-flavonoids seem favourably to alter the way our bodies use vitamin C. It helps concentrate the nutrient in various tissues making it more absorbable, according to the American Journal of Clinical Nutrition.

BIRTH CONTROL PILLS

Users Need More Vitamin B-6 and Folic Acid. Research has shown that women taking the birth control pill are often low in the vital nutrient vitamin B-6. The National Research Council reported that 15% to 20% of oral contraceptive users show signs of B-6 deficiency.

Birth control pill users also need more folic acid, part of the B-complex vitamins, according to Dr Daphne Roe, Professor of Nutrition at Cornell University. Foods high in vitamin B-6 include whole grain cereals, wheat germ, vegetables, bananas and meat. Good sources of folic acid include leafy, dark green vegetables, organ meats and citrus fruits.

When taking the pill, be sure your diet provides enough B-6 and folic acid. If you're not sure consider vitamin supplements.

BLISTERS ON FEET

What To Do For Blisters.
- Wash the blister thoroughly with soap and water. Let dry.
- Apply a plaster strip to the blister. Apply other overlapping plaster until the entire blister and a margin of normal skin is smoothly covered with tape.
- Leave this in place for five days then remove. The dead surface of skin of the blister usually hangs limp by this time. You can trim it off with scissors or let it dry.

BLOATING

Suggestions For Relieving Bloating. Many women before their menstrual period find themselves puffy and water-logged. Clothes fit too tightly due to temporary gain in water weight. This can be very uncomfortable. The following tips will help avoid bloating:

- Reduce salt intake. Buy a salt substitute or flavour foods with lemon juice, herbs and spices. Avoid salty snack foods like potato crisps. Carefully check food labels for excess salt content.
- Stay away from foods that cause intestinal gas. Most common offenders are dairy products, nuts and spicy foods like pizza and tacos.

- Avoid cola drinks and chocolate.
- Keep your weight down. Excess fat tissue attracts and stores fluid.
- Avoid emotional stress.
- Avoid alcohol. It makes bloating worse, especially on hot days.
- Wear loose clothing. Avoid belts and tight shoes. Also wear low-heeled shoes. Take off tight rings if your hands swell.
- Avoid water pills. Water pills cause your kidneys to work overtime leading to a loss of important minerals such as potassium, sodium, calcium and magnesium, according to Dr Milan Pazourek of Tacoma, Washington.
- Drink more water. Drinking four to six glasses of water a day makes your kidneys work more efficiently.
- Exercising improves vascular tone and circulation.
- Eat natural diuretics like water-melon, strawberries, apples, grapes, beets, asparagus. They stimulate the body to eliminate water.
- Take vitamin B-6. You can take up to 200 mg a day during times of pre-menstrual fluid retention. This helps reduce bloating.
- Eat only fish or protein for two or three meals a day. This will have a diuretic effect on the body.

Three ingredients were found safe and effective as diuretics by a US government panel of medical experts:

- Ammonium chloride (should not be used by anyone with impaired kidney or liver function). Effectiveness diminishes after four or five days.
- Pamabrom.
- Caffeine.
  You should use diuretics only when all other measures fail to bring relief.

BLOOD PRESSURE

What Is Blood Pressure? Blood pressure is the force of the blood against artery walls which carry blood through the body. Blood pressure is measured using two numbers. The first number is your systolic pressure. This is the larger number. It measures the force of your blood against artery walls when the heart has contracted and is gushing blood through the body. Think of the systolic pressure as a garden hose measuring the force in your arteries when the water is turned on. The second number measures the diastolic pressure. This is the force of the blood against the arteries when the heart is resting between beats. Think of the diastolic number as measuring the pressure in your arteries when the garden hose is turned off. So if your blood pressure is 140/70, it means that your blood is exerting 140 pounds of pressure against your artery walls when your heart contracts and 70 pounds of pressure when your heart rests. Normal blood pressure is around 120/80.

High Blood Pressure. Most doctors would consider regular blood pressure readings over about 140/90 to be high.

High blood pressure has been called the silent disease since it very often has no symptoms. However, over time the excessive force exerted on the artery walls may damage the arteries, kidneys, heart and brain, leading to heart attacks or strokes.

The specific cause of high blood pressure is not known. But doctors know what makes it worse. Too much salt in the diet, being overweight, lack of exercise and emotional stress may worsen the situation.

Diagnosing High Blood Pressure. High blood pressure must be diagnosed over a period of time by taking regular readings. Everyone goes through blood pressure swings throughout the day. It is not uncommon for blood pressure counts to have a 30-point variance in a short period of time. Because of this, high blood pressure can be difficult to diagnose.

Having your blood pressure taken at the doctor's surgery can often make your blood pressure soar and lead to an incorrect diagnosis, says Bill Sanders of the National Heart, Lung and Blood Institute. This is commonly called the "white coat" syndrome, where a patient gets very anxious in a doctor's surgery while having a physical examination. Be sure that any diagnosis of high blood pressure is based on a series of readings over time.

Calcium. According to a study published in the American Journal of Clinical Nutrition, high blood pressure was reduced in women who took regular calcium supplements. All of the women were taking high blood pressure medication. By supplementing their diet with calcium for a year, blood pressure readings - especially the higher systolic pressure - were reduced significantly. Other women who had normal blood pressure and who supplemented their diet with calcium showed no change in their blood pressure. Women having elevated blood pressure should consider supplementing their diet with about 1,000 mg of calcium daily.

Fibre. A high-fibre diet can lower blood pressure by about 10%, says Dr James Anderson, Professor of Medicine and Clinical Nutrition at the University of Kentucky. After examining the effects of fibre on blood pressure and cholesterol levels on hundreds of patients for ten years, it was found that fibre, such as oats, beans and other vegetables, lowers blood pressure (and cholesterol).

Potassium. A low potassium diet has been shown by various studies to increase the incidence of high blood pressure.

Bio-Feed Back. Dr Alan Jacobson of the University of Miami School of Medicine says that bio-feed back can lower blood pressure. Basically, there are three stages of bio-feed back training:

- The patient is hooked up to a machine that measures the level of muscle tension, letting him see the degree of tension on the bio-feed machine.
- The machine tells the patient when muscle tension drops or increases. In this way the patient is able to see how tense muscles elevate blood pressure.
- The patient is then taught how to calm the tense muscles to keep blood pressure under control. Bio-feed back training has helped hundreds of people suffering from high blood pressure to reduce their level to normal.

Low-Fat Diet. Nathan Pritikin, the famous advocate of the low-fat diet, says that excessive fat in the diet is the main cause of high blood pressure. He believes that fat and oil intake cause red blood cells to bunch up and stick together. These clumps of blood cells are unable to pass through the smaller vessels of the circulatory system, acting as "little corks" blocking circulation at thousands of locations through the body. When this happens pressure of the blood flowing in the body becomes elevated. With a low-fat diet the blood cells become "unclumped". The circulatory system expands and pressure drops.

In his two books "The Pritikin Promise" and "The Pritikin Programme For Diet and Exercise", Nathan Pritikin documents dozens of cases where persons suffering high blood pressure were able to reduce significantly blood pressure readings and get off blood pressure medication.

Mackerel. An interesting experiment was carried out by West German researchers at the Central Institute for Cardiovascular Research. Men with mild hypertension were given two tins of mackerel with tomatoes every day for two weeks. The result was a significant lowering of their blood pressure. When the mackerel intake was reduced to three cans a week, their blood pressure stayed low until the men reverted to eating cold meats and little fish.

Regular Check-ups. High blood pressure may develop suddenly and without warning. Unless you have regular check-ups you may have elevated blood pressure for years without knowing it. High blood pressure is treatable with medication or simple life style changes. Have your blood pressure checked regularly.

BLOWING YOUR NOSE

The Proper Way To Blow Your Nose. There is a proper way to blow your nose to avoid problems with your ear drums. Blow your nose gently, keeping mouth open. If both nostrils are clogged, blow them at the same time, keeping your mouth open. Do not blow each nostril separately.

BODY ODOUR

5 Tips To Get Rid Of. Body odour is caused by an interaction of bacteria and sweat. Many people suffer body odour despite good personal hygiene. This can cause serious social problems. These recommendations may help avoid body odour:

- Magnesium taken together with zinc, paba and vitamin B-6 can control offensive body odours, according to Dr B F Hart, a physician practising in Fort Lauderdale, Florida.
- Don't bathe every day with soap and water. Twice a week is sufficient. Daily bathing washes away natural body oils that lubricate and protect skin from bacteria.

- Use an antibiotic ointment (neomycin solution 0.5%) under arms daily after washing.
- Bathe rectal and genital areas and feet daily.
- Don't use commercial deodorants that prevent perspiration. They stop waste products from leaving the body.

BOILS

5 Home Care Suggestions. Boils are caused by staphylococci bacteria that enter the skin through a hair follicle. It develops into a pus-filled pocket that comes to a head and finally drains.

- Never squeeze a boil. Most boils rupture and heal on their own. Squeezing may force infection into the blood stream.
- Apply moist heat. Hold a soft cloth soaked with warm water on the boil for 15 minutes, four times a day. This will hasten draining.
- The bacteria in the boil is contagious. Disinfect the cloth by boiling or washing in hot water.
- When boil ruptures wash affected area thoroughly and cover with an antibiotic cream and gauze.
- Boils near nose or ears or accompanied by fever should be examined by a doctor promptly.

Zinc For Boil Flareups. Supplementing the diet with zinc may help stop boils. Dr Isser Brody of Sweden noticed that 15 of his patients with a chronic boil problem had low blood levels of zinc. He gave eight of the patients 45 mg of zinc, three times a day for about three months. Blood zinc levels rose to normal and no new boils occurred. The other seven patients did not take zinc and continued to suffer recurring boils.

Foods high in zinc include liver, meats, turkey, soya beans, seafood and whole grains.

BREAST CANCER

Minimising Chance Of Problems. Breast cancer is most common in women between the ages of 44 and 55. It is linked to people who are overweight and eat a high fat diet. Breast cancer is treatable if detected early. Over 65% of the victims are still alive after five years.

Symptoms Of Breast Cancer.
- A lump or thickness with persistent soreness.
- A discharge from the nipple.
- A lump in the armpit.
- Any sensitive area in the breast.
- Any change in skin colour or texture especially redness accompanying itching and dimpling of the skin.

Risk Factors. Women having the highest risk factors fall into the following categories.

- Women over 40.
- A family history of cancer in females (mother, grandmother, sister, aunt).
- Prior history of benign tumours or other cancer.
- Little sexual activity.
- No pregnancies or having a child after age 35.
- Mothers who did not nurse their babies.
- Long term oestrogen users or users of oral contraceptives.
- Obesity.

Preventative Measures.
- Read the section of this book under Cancer Risk for information on how you can lower your chances of getting cancer.
- Have an annual check-up, especially if you are in a high risk category.
- Avoid oestrogen therapy.
- Lose weight if you need to.
- Do not smoke.
- Reduce the caffeine in your diet.
- Do a monthly breast self-examination.

Breast Self-Examination. Breast self-examination should be done once a month so you become familiar with the usual appearance and feel of your breasts. Familiarity makes it easier to notice any changes in the breast from one month to another. Early discovery of a change from what is "normal" is the main idea behind Breast Self-Examination.

The following breast self-examination is recommended:

1. Stand before a mirror. Inspect both breasts for anything unusual, such as any discharge from the nipples, puckering, dimpling, or scaling of the skin.
2. Watching closely in the mirror, clasp hands behind your head and press hands forward.
3. Next, press hands firmly on hips and bow slightly toward your mirror as you pull your shoulders and elbows forward.
4. Raise your left arm. Use three or four fingers of your right hand to explore your left breast firmly, carefully and thoroughly. Beginning at the outer edge, press the flat part of your fingers in small circles, moving the circles slowly around the breast. Gradually work toward the nipple. Be sure to cover the entire breast. Pay special attention to the area between the breast and the armpit, including the armpit itself. Feel for any unusual lump or mass under the skin.
5. Gently squeeze the nipple and look for a discharge. Repeat the examination on your right breast.

BRONCHITIS

Supplementing Medical Care. Bronchitis is an inflammation of the bronchial tubes. It may be caused by a viral or bacterial infection. Many persons get bronchitis time and again.

- *Vitamin A.* 7,500 IUs (International Units) daily may help medical treatment by stimulating the mucous membrane upper respiratory tract to resist infections. Foods rich in vitamin A include broccoli, carrots, fish, green and yellow fruits and low-fat milk.
- *Vitamin C.* 500 to 1,000 mg a day may increase resistance to bacterial or viral infections. Foods rich in vitamin C include citrus fruits and fruit juices, berries, cabbage, green vegetables and potatoes.

BRUISES

Avoiding Bruises. Bruises are caused from breaks in the small blood vessels in the soft tissues beneath the skin. These breaks leak blood which cause a reddish mark on the surface of the skin. This bruise mark turns bluish then yellowish as the blood leak is gradually absorbed.

Vitamin C. Several research studies have shown vitamin C helps strengthen the capillary walls. People who bruise easily can often prevent many bruises by supplementing their diet with vitamin C. Foods rich in vitamin C include citrus fruits and fruit juices, berries, cabbage, green vegetables and potatoes.

Zinc. People having low zinc levels were found to bruise easily, according to clinical research studies. Dr Dean Edell, a prominent San Diego physician, recommends taking 30 mg of zinc daily if you bruise easily.

BURNED TONGUE

How To Relieve. Sprinkle a few grains of sugar on the tongue burn. Reapply as necessary. Pain should subside in minutes.

BURNS

First Degree Burns. A first degree burn results in damage to the outer layer of the skin only. Some common first degree burns: sunburn, contact with hot objects, hot water or steam.

Symptoms.
- Redness.
- Mild swelling.
- Pain.
- Unbroken skin with no blisters.

What To Do.

Place the burned area under cold, running water and apply cold water compress such as a clean towel or face cloth. Do this until pain subsides. Cover the burn with clean bandages. Do not apply butter or grease to a burn. Do not apply other medications without a doctor's recommendation.

Second Degree Burns. This is a burn that causes injury to skin beneath the surface of the body. Some common second degree burns include deep sunburn, hot liquids and burns from petrol and other substances.

Symptoms.
- Redness or blotchy appearance to burn.
- Blisters.
- Swelling lasting several days.
- Moist, oozing appearance to the surface of the skin.
- Pain.

What To Do.
- Place burned area under cold water (not iced) or apply cold water compress such as a clean towel or face cloth until pain subsides.
- Gently pat area with dry towel or other soft material.
- Cover burned area with a dry, sterile bandage or clean cloth to prevent infection.
- Elevate burned arms or legs.
- Seek medical attention.

Third Degree Burns. This kind of burn destroys all layers of the skin. Common third degree burns include prolonged contact with fire, hot substances or electrical burns.

Symptoms.
- Burned area is white or charred.
- Skin is destroyed.
- There is little pain because nerve endings have been destroyed.

What To Do.
- Do not remove clothes that are stuck to burn.

- Do not put ice or water on burns.
- Do not apply ointment, sprays or antiseptics.
- Consult a doctor immediately.

4 Tips For Preventing Burns.
- Never smoke in bed or when drowsy.
- When cooking, don't wear loosely fitting, flammable clothing. Bathrobes, night-gowns and pyjamas can catch fire.
- Set water heater thermostats or taps so that water does not scald the skin.
- Plan which emergency exists to use in case of fire.

BURSITIS

Relieving Pain. This is a pain caused by inflammation in the bursae - the small sacs located at the ends of the bones in the joints. These sacs contain lubricating fluids that eliminate friction. The inflammation can result from a sudden pressure or prolonged strain. Common areas of bursitis are the shoulder, elbow, hip, knee and ankle. Tips for easing pain:

- Rest the area affected.
- Apply ice to the painful area three or four times a day for up to 20 minutes at a time.
- After about two days replace the ice treatment with heat treatments. Heat treatments can be with hot pack or heating pads. Or simply take a hot shower. If the pain continues consult a physician.

CALORIES USED

The following list shows the calories used per hour for various kinds of daily activities.

Activity	Calories per hour
Dancing	330
Bicycling (at 5.5 miles per hour)	210
Bowling	264
Desk work	408
Driving a car	168
Gardening	220
Golf	300
Netball	612
Horse riding	480
Mowing the lawn	462
Cooking a meal	198
Roller-skating	350
Running at 10 miles per hour	900
Sitting and eating	84
Skiing	594
Sleeping	60
Swimming	300
Tennis	350
Volleyball	350

CANCER RISK

Cancer On The Increase. The American Cancer Society says the number of people expected to get cancer is up - from 1 in 4 for those born in 1970 to 1 in 3 for those born in 1985. One reason: longer lives increase the risk of cancer. Cancer is the second major cause of death in the US after heart disease.

Lowering The Risk of Cancer. Substantial scientific evidence shows that many cancers are linked to the foods we eat. By eating the right kinds of foods you can reduce the risk of cancer. The American Institute for Cancer Research has published dietary guidelines for lowering the risks of cancer. Here is what the Institute recommends:

1. Reduce the intake of fat, both saturated and unsaturated. Americans currently average about 40% of total calories from fat. This level should be reduced to 30% of total calorie intake.
2. Increase the consumption of fruits, vegetables and whole grains.
3. Consume less salt-cured, smoked and charcoal broiled foods.
4. Drink alcoholic beverages only in moderation.

Hints For Controlling Fat Intake. Fat is a valuable part of our diet. It provides energy and essential fatty acids, vitamin D and E. However, most people consume more fat than is necessary.

Research suggests that high-fat eating habits are associated with greater risk of cancer. Here are some tips for reducing fat intake:

- Meat is a major source of fat in our diets. Limit the size of meat portions to 6 ounces per day. Choose lean meats rather than meats that are fatty. Limit use of sausage and luncheon meats.
- Trim fat from meat and skin from poultry.
- Substitute low-fat dairy products for those high in fat. Use skimmed milk instead of whole milk. Use low-fat yoghurt or imitation sour cream instead of real sour cream. Try evaporated skimmed milk in recipes that call for heavy cream. Use low-fat cheese instead of high-fat cheese. Low-fat cheeses include cottage cheese, part-skim mozzarella and ricotta. High-fat cheeses include Cheddar, cream and Swiss.
- Read labels carefully. Non-dairy products labelled no cholesterol may still contain large amounts of fat. Choose foods that are labelled as low-fat or contain low-fat items in the list of ingredients.
- Limit fat in cooking. Bake or broil meat - don't fry. Use a rack in the pan when cooking meats to allow fat to drip out. Poach food in water or broth instead of sautéing it. Use non-stick pans to eliminate the need for fat in cooking. Steam vegetables quickly instead of cooking them in fat.
- Use only small amounts of regular salad dressing.

- Adjust baked goods recipes by using one-half to three-quarters the amount of fat recommended.
- Nuts and seeds are naturally high in fat. Eat them sparingly.
- Choose low-fat, high nutrient snacks like fresh fruit, raw vegetables, popcorn and whole grain. Limit intake of potato crisps, chocolate and ice cream.

Eat More Whole Grains. Whole grains should be eaten several times a day. Below are some ways you can use whole grains.

- Substitute whole wheat flour for all-purpose flour in recipes for baked products.
- Check ingredients on ready-made bread to ensure that the first ingredient listed is whole grain.
- Use brown rice in place of white rice for greater nutritional value. One cup of uncooked brown rice cooked in two cups of water for 50 minutes yields about four cups of cooked rice.
- Use barley in soup or as a side dish. Whole grain barley is more nutritious than pearly barley. To serve barley as a side dish bring it to the boil in about three parts water, then cover and simmer 30 to 50 minutes until the barley is tender and the water is absorbed.
- Millet is a light-textured, mild-flavoured grain. It can replace rice in most recipes. It should be steamed in two-and-a-half parts liquid for about 20 minutes.
- For breakfast select cereals that have whole grain products first in the list of ingredients.
- Whole grain foods like popcorn or rye crackers are excellent snacks that provide more nutrients and fewer calories than potato crisps.

Eat More Foods Rich In Vitamin A and C. Consumption of foods high in beta-carotene (which is converted to vitamin A after consumption) and vitamin C has been associated with lower rates of some cancers. Certain fruits and vegetables are the best source of these nutrients. They provide high levels of other vitamins and minerals in addition to beta-carotene and vitamin C. They are also good sources of dietary fibre. Consume them as frequently as possible.

- The best sources of beta-carotene are dark green and deep yellow fruits and vegetables. These fruits include apricots, cantaloup, nectarines, papayas and water-melon. Vegetables high in beta-carotenes include broccoli, carrots, sweet potatoes and all dark, leafy vegetables such as spinach and chard.
- Vitamin C-rich fruits include cantaloup, grapefruit, oranges and strawberries. The best vegetable sources of vitamin C are broccoli, cabbage, peppers and tomato juice.
- Try eating vegetables raw or cooked quickly by steaming or stir-frying. They stay crispier and have more flavour. Less of the nutrients are destroyed with rapid cooking.
- Try salads made of dark greens such as spinach or non-leafy vegetables such as green peppers, carrots, broccoli, tomatoes and cauliflower.
- Marinate cut-up vegetables in a container with lemon juice or vinegar, herbs and spices. Serve them with meals or as snacks.
- Increase the amount of vegetables in meat-vegetable casseroles while decreasing the amount of meat. Remember large amounts of meat are unnecessary and contribute extra fat to the diet.
- Try the natural sweetness of fruit instead of biscuits or sweets.
- Substitute fruit or vegetable juices for tea, coffee and fizzy drinks.

Hints For Increasing Use Of Pulses. Dried pulses such as lentils, beans and peas are a major part of the diet of many foreign countries. Unfortunately, we don't eat enough of them. Such pulses can make a valuable contribution to our diets. They are good sources of protein, iron, magnesium, zinc and several B vitamins. They are high in dietary fibre. For these reasons many health professionals are encouraging increased consumption of pulses.

- Dried beans, peas, chickpeas and lentils can be combined with other ingredients in soups, salads and stews. They can also be served alone, flavoured with herbs and other seasonings. Some people like them puréed and made into sandwich spreads and dips. Tofu (soya bean curd) can be cut into cubes and substituted for all or part of the chicken in many casserole or Oriental recipes.
- Soaking and cooking. One cup of dried beans, peas or lentils expands to two or two-and-a-half cups after cooking. Dried beans must be pre-soaked using either the overnight or quick method. The overnight method: wash

beans and place in four parts water, cover and let stand eight hours. Quick method: bring water and beans to the boil and cook for 2 minutes. Cover, remove from heat and let stand for 1 hour. After pre-soaking by either method boil beans gently for 1.5 to 2 hours until soft. If you use a pressure cooker, beans can be cooked in 3 to 10 minutes after pre-soaking or in 25 to 45 minutes without pre-soaking.

Be sure to follow package directions carefully because cooking times may vary with the type of beans. Lentils do not need pre-soaking and cook in 30 minutes. If salt is added don't use it until the beans are nearly tender. Salt toughens bean skins and slows cooking. Cooked beans can be stored in the refrigerator for one week or in the freezer for several months.

National Cancer Institute Suggestions For Lowering Cancer Risk.

- Don't smoke cigarettes, pipes or cigars. Don't chew tobacco or use snuff.
- Avoid too much sunlight, particularly if you are fair skinned. Use sun screens and wear protective clothing.
- Don't ask for an X-ray if your doctor or dentist does not recommend it. If you need an X-ray be sure X-ray shields are used to protect other parts of your body.
- If you are exposed to work place carcinogens, reduce exposure by wearing proper safety clothing.

Colon Cancer: Reducing The Risk. Results of a 20 year study published in the medical journal, Lancet, showed that a diet rich in calcium and vitamin D may help reduce the risk of colon cancer.

The study involved almost 2,000 men. Those men consuming ample amounts of calcium and vitamin D in their diets had almost two-thirds less colon cancer than men consuming low amounts of these nutrients.

Preliminary findings show that consuming about 1,200 mg of calcium and about 350 IUs of vitamin D each day may significantly cut the risk of colon cancer.

Dr Paul Rozen, of the Tel Aviv Medical Centre, found that calcium, taken in amounts 50% greater than recommended minimums, suppressed the rapid growth of mucosal cells in the colon, which are thought to be a risk to cancer formation. While Dr Rozen said that further research was needed, he saw no problem with people increasing the calcium in their diet, as long as they did not increase fat intake.

Drinking an 8 oz glass of skimmed milk, four times a day provides ample amounts of calcium and vitamin D. Other good sources of these nutrients include cottage cheese, low-fat yoghurt, salmon and broccoli.

Aspirin. A study carried out at Memorial Sloan-Kettering Cancer Centre in New York, together with Boston University, Cornell Medical Centre and the University of Pennsylvania, found that people who take aspirin at least four times a week are 50% less likely to develop colon or rectal cancer. Apparently, aspirin could inhibit the development of substances called prostaglandins which aid the growth of tumours.

Stomach Cancer. A preliminary study in China, co-sponsored by the National Cancer Institute in America, found that vegetables from the Allium family (onions, garlic, scallions, chives) may reduce the risk of stomach cancer. Of the people in the survey who ate the onion-type vegetables, most had their stomach cancer risk cut to 40% of the risk of those who rarely ate such vegetables.

Another study in Hawaii showed that people who ate onions more than 21 times a month made their cancer risk three times lower than people who only ate them eight times in a month. The effective ingredient in onions is quercetin and doctors still have a lot of work to do on it.

CAUSES OF DEATH

10 Worst Killers Of Americans. The ten leading causes of death in the United States are as follows:

1. Heart disease.
2. Cancer.
3. Stroke.
4. Accidents.
5. Lung disease.
6. Pneumonia and influenza.
7. Diabetes.
8. Cirrhosis of the liver.
9. Circulatory disease.
10. Suicide.

Most major causes of death are closely associated with diet - especially cancer, heart disease and stroke. Most lung disease is caused by excessive cigarette smoking. Cirrhosis of the liver is mostly caused by excessive alcohol consumption.

CELLULITE

Just Plain Fat. Cellulite are those bumpy, cottage cheese-like globs of fat that are around your thighs and stomach. These ugly, orange-peel pits and dimples are just fat, according to Dr Neil Solomon of Johns-Hopkins University in Baltimore, Maryland.

- Dr Solomon took samples of cellulite and fat. He found no difference whatsoever in the cells of each. Cellulite and fat are exactly the same.
- Fat and cellulite occur on the body for the same reasons. Excess calories are not burned off and turn to fat.
- The only way to get rid of cellulite is through diet and exercise.

CHAFING

Tips For Relieving Chafing.
- Apply hydrocortisone cream sparingly, twice a day for three to four days.
- Apply zinc oxide ointment twice a day then clean it with baby or mineral oil.
- Applying baby powder to the skin may protect sensitive areas from chafing.

CHOKING

What To Do When You're Alone.
- When you start to choke make a fist with the thumb curled outside.
- Place your fist, thumb side, against your abdomen slightly above the naval and below the rib cage.
- Then grasp your fist with your free hand and press it in your abdomen with a quick upper thrust.

- Repeat the manoeuvre until the foreign object is expelled. This is called the Heimlich manoeuvre developed by Dr Henry Heimlich. You can perform the manoeuvre standing, sitting or even lying down.

CHOLESTEROL (See Also HEART DISEASE)

Cause Of Heart Disease And Stroke. Cholesterol is a fat-like, pearly substance found in saturated animal fats and oils. Foods high in cholesterol include egg yokes, cream, butter, cheese and fatty meats. The normal blood cholesterol level ranges from 150 to 250 mg per decilitre. Many specialists recommend keeping cholesterol levels below 200. Some specialists recommend keeping it under 150.

Many studies have shown that high cholesterol levels increase your risk of heart attack and stroke. Here's how doctors say cholesterol damages your body. Cholesterol is carried in the blood stream where some is deposited in the inner linings of the arteries. These fatty deposits build up causing the artery walls to thicken and become less flexible. The artery narrows and restricts blood flow. Eventually, the blood supply may be shut off completely. If the blood stoppage is in an artery feeding the brain a stroke may result. If the clogged artery feeds the heart, a heart attack may occur.

Reducing Cholesterol In Your Diet.
- Choose lean meat, fish, poultry, dried beans and peas as protein sources.
- Moderate use of eggs and organ meats such as liver and kidneys.
- Use skimmed or low-fat milk.
- Limit intake of butter, cream, shortenings, coconut oil and foods made from such products.
- Eat less sausage, bacon and processed luncheon meats.
- Trim excess fat off meats.
- Broil, bake and boil rather than fry.
- Read labels carefully to determine amounts and type of fat in foods.

Fat In Your Diet - Saturated And Unsaturated. Saturated fat is usually hard at room temperature. For example, fat on cooked beef becomes hard and white if left out at room temperature. The major sources of saturated fat in our diets are meat and dairy products. Saturated fat intake is a strong contributor to raising blood cholesterol levels.

Polyunsaturated fat stays soft or in liquid form at room temperature. All vegetable oils are rich in polyunsaturated fat and have no cholesterol. Polyunsaturated fat will lower blood cholesterol, according to the National Heart, Lung and Blood Institute in America.

The chart below shows the percentage of polyunsaturated fat and saturated fat for various types of oil or fat. When you use oils or fats choose those high in polyunsaturated fat - the ones at the top of the chart.

Type of Oil or Fat	Percentage Polyunsaturated Fat	Percentage Saturated Fat
Safflower Oil	74%	9%
Sunflower Oil	64%	10%
Corn Oil	58%	13%
Average Vegetable Oil (soya oil plus rapeseed)	36%	9%
Peanut Oil	30%	19%
Chicken Fat (Schmaltz)	26%	29%
Average Vegetable Shortening	20%	32%
Lard	12%	40%
Olive Oil	9%	14%
Beef Fat	4%	48%
Butter	4%	48%
Palm Oil	2%	81%
Coconut Oil	2%	86%

When You're At Risk.

Cholesterol (in mg per decilitre)		
Age	**Moderate Risk**	**High Risk**
2-19	Over 170	Over 185
20-29	Over 200	Over 220
30-39	Over 220	Over 240
40 and up	Over 240	Over 260

COCKROACHES

Killing With Boric Acid. Cockroaches can contaminate your home with germs and promote disease. To kill cockroaches, sprinkle boric acid on to skirting boards and crevices in the kitchen. This is a time-proven remedy that will kill cockroaches within six days. They will not develop a resistance to boric acid as they do with commercial products. Boric acid is safer than commercial products. It is not toxic to children. It is not absorbed into the skin and not easily inhaled.

COFFEE

Greater Risk Of Heart Attack. A Stanford University study showed that coffee increases the level of certain types of cholesterol in the blood. Men drinking two cups of coffee or more a day face a higher risk of heart disease. Coffee should be drunk only in moderation, say researchers.

COLD (COMMON)

Try Zinc To Shorten Misery. Zinc can reduce the time you will be affected by a common cold, says Dr Jeffrey Fisher, Medical Director of the Extensis Medical Centre in Roslyn, New York. Zinc appears to kill the viruses that cause the common cold. Zinc won't prevent a cold, but it can stimulate the body's infection-fighting defences - thus reducing the time a cold will make you miserable.

- Zinc was tested on 65 volunteers suffering from colds. 37 were given zinc. Those individuals suffered only 3.7 days. The other volunteers were given a fake pill. They suffered an average of 10.8 days - almost three times longer.
- The dosage of zinc was 23 mg of zinc (gluconate) every 2 hours with a maximum dosage of 12 tablets or 250 mg.
- The zinc tablets should not be swallowed. They have to be sucked over a period of about 10 minutes.
- The zinc should not be taken for more than one week. It may upset the balance of copper in your system and upset the immune system.
- Pre-sweetened lozenges available at most health food shops are recommended. If not available suck zinc tablets along with a sweet mint to mask the zinc taste. Consult your doctor before taking zinc supplements.

Vitamin C. Vitamin C may help shorten the duration of a common cold, according to a study published in the Medical Journal of Australia. The study involved 95 pairs of twins. One of each pair of twins took 100 mg of vitamin C for 100 days. The other twins took a fake pill. Twins taking the vitamin C recovered from cold symptoms 19% sooner. Foods rich in vitamin C include citrus fruits, fruit juices, berries, cabbage, green vegetables and potatoes.

Other Helpful Suggestions.
- Stay in bed if possible.
- Take aspirin or paracetamol. Don't take aspirin with vitamin C. The combination may increase stomach irritation.
- Do not smoke - stay away from others who do smoke. Cigarette smoking weakens resistance and lung power.
- Avoid complications by staying away from crowds.
- Eat properly and consult your doctor if condition worsens.

COLD SORES

Home Remedies. Cold sores are caused by the herpes simplex virus. This virus affects about 85% of the population. Some doctors believe it is the second most common ailment - next to the common cold.

The cold sore starts as a tiny, painful red spot generally on the lip or corner of the mouth. These sores form a blister that turns into a scab. This scab lasts from a week to a fortnight. Many people regularly suffer cold sores. Cold sores can be transmitted by hugging, kissing and other direct contact. Try these suggestions for cold sore relief:

- *Vitamin E.* Dr Don Nead, a dentist from Redding, California, uses vitamin E to treat cold sores. He recommends applying 20,000 IUs for about 15 minutes, three times a day. This relieves or eliminates cold sore pain in less than eight hours. The sore actually heals itself in 12 to 24 hours in many cases. Dr Nead reports an almost 100% success rate with this method.
- *Ice.* This ancient remedy really helps. According to several physicians, cold sores are best treated by holding an ice cube directly on the erupted cold sore for 45 minutes. This is more effective and cheaper than any other drug treatment. One physician said cold sores usually dry up in a day or two after ice cube treatments.
- *Lysine.* Cold sores can also be successfully treated with the amino acid lysine, says Christopher Kagan of Cedar-Sinai Medical Centre in Los Angeles, California. Lysine counteracts the production of the herpes virus, he believes. He conducted a study on 25 persons suffering from recurring cold sores. They were given 800 to 1,000 mg of lysine each day. The patients reported less pain, faster healing and less frequent recurrence of the cold sores. Lysine is available at health food stores.

  In another study, researchers at Indiana University gave lysine to 250 patients suffering cold sores. The dosage ranged from 312 to 1,200 mg daily. Only 2% of the subjects showed no improvement. Researchers say if lysine is taken at first sign of stinging pain an attack may be averted.
- *Yoghurt.* Dr Morton Malkin, a dentist from Brooklyn, New York, recommends yoghurt for cold sores. Yoghurt contains lactobacillus acidophilus (or lactobacillus bulgaricus). The doctor believes these good bacteria crowd out the herpes cold sores in the body. He also recommends high

doses of vitamin B-complex and increased fluid intake. Hundreds of patients have been treated with this method.

COMPUTER EYE STRAIN

Tips To Avoid. Eye strain caused by using a computer is very common, causing symptoms such as headache, blurred vision and burning eyes, says Dr R Anthony Hutchinson of San Diego, California. Follow these rules to avoid problems:

- Position yourself about 22 inches from the screen.
- Get rid of glare reflecting off your computer screen.
- Blink your eyes periodically.
- Take scheduled breaks from the computer.
- Have your eyes examined to make sure you do not need glasses. Make sure you have the proper prescription.

CONSTIPATION

Conditions That Can Cause. It is not necessary to have a bowel movement every day. From three bowel movements each day to three each week is considered normal. Constipation can be accompanied by fatigue, bloatiness and mild cramps. The following can cause constipation:

- Diets low in fibre or roughage and high in animal fat.
- Stress can lead to constipation. Also certain drugs, including antacids and pain relievers, can cause problems.
- Travel can cause constipation. This is due to changes in drinking water, diet and daily activities.
- Older people sometimes suffer constipation because of not drinking enough fluids, lack of exercise and low fibre diets.
- Pregnancy.
- Over-use of laxatives resulting in dependence is a common cause.

Suggestions For Avoiding Constipation.
- Eat fruit, raw vegetables, bran, high bulk foods, whole grain bread and whole grain cereals.
- Eat regularly.
- Get plenty of physical exercise.
- Drink a half glass of hot water half an hour before breakfast every day.
- Drink a total of eight glasses of fluids daily - two should be prune juice.
- Never strain. Be relaxed.
- Have regular bowel movements at the same time of day. The best time is half an hour or so after breakfast.
- If you're still having difficulty add an ounce of mineral oil to fruit juice and drink before going to bed.

Try Yoghurt And Prunes. A study published in the Journal of the American Medical Association showed that a mixture of yoghurt and prunes helps constipation. The study involved 194 patients suffering constipation. Nearly all the participants experienced relief by taking a mixture of yoghurt and prunes. Researchers believe the lactobacillus acid ophilus in yoghurt helps promote regularity.

Try Popcorn. An effective remedy, particularly for constipation in children, is to eat a large packet or two of popcorn daily, according to Dr James McKay, professor of paediatrics at the University of Vermont. It works because popcorn is very bulky which means it absorbs and holds water, making the stool soft.

CONTACT LENSES

Common Problems With Contact Lenses.
- *Bacterial Infection.* If the infection is serious it can leave scars on your eye and decrease vision. The most common cause of infection is poor hygiene - especially when surface of cornea is scratched, says Dr R Linsy Farris.
- *Scratches.* Scratched cornea on inner eyelid can also turn to infection.
- *Allergic Reactions.* This can be caused by chemicals used to clean the lenses.

- *Discomfort.* Pain can result from abrasions on the cornea caused by wearing hard contact lenses too long.

Protecting Yourself From Injury.
- Make sure you are examined by a qualified optician.
- Have regular follow-up examinations.
- Be sure you understand how to insert and remove your lenses.
- Learn proper hygiene techniques from your optician.

CONTRACEPTIVES

Comparing The Options. A number of contraception methods are available today. Some can be obtained without a doctor's prescription or advice. Others require a prescription, medical consultation and follow-up.

Basic information on the contraceptive methods most widely used is given below. This is only essential information to help you understand the choices available. Discussion with a physician can help you make a selection that is right for you.

No method of contraception is 100% effective. Correct use of a method is essential to ensure maximum effectiveness. The more care taken in using a method exactly as instructed, the more effective it will be. Using a combination of methods (such as diaphragm and condom, foam and condom, etc) will also increase the contraceptive effectiveness.

The Pill. "The Pill" refers to any of the oral contraceptives. The most widely used contains two female hormones, oestrogen and progestin - taken 21 days each month. Another (sometimes called the "mini-pill") contains progestin only and is taken continuously. Full instructions come with your prescription on the use, benefits and risks of the product.

Effectiveness of the Pill.
- Effectiveness depends on how correctly the method is used. Of 100 women who use the combination oestrogen and progestin pill for one year, less than one will become pregnant. Of 100 women who use the progestin-only pill (mini-pill) for one year, two to three will become pregnant.

Advantages.

- The combination pill is the most effective of all popular methods of preventing pregnancy.
- No inconvenient devices to bother with at time of intercourse.

Disadvantages.

- Must be taken regularly and exactly as instructed.

Side Effects.

- Side effects may include tender breasts, nausea, vomiting, gain or loss of weight, unexpected vaginal bleeding, higher levels of sugar and fat in the blood.
- Although it happens infrequently, use of the Pill can cause blood clots (in the legs, and less frequently in the lungs, brain and heart). A clot that reaches the lungs or forms in the brain or heart can be fatal. Pill users have a greater risk of heart attack and stroke than non-users. This risk increases with age and is greater if the Pill user smokes.
- Some Pill users tend to develop high blood pressure. It usually is mild and may be reversed by discontinuing use.
- Pill users have a greater risk than non-users of having gall bladder disease requiring surgery.
- There is no substantial evidence that taking the Pill increases the risk of cancer. Rarely, benign liver tumours occur in women on the Pill. Sometimes they rupture causing fatal haemorrhage.

Health Factors to Consider.

- Women who use the Pill are strongly advised not to smoke because smoking increases the risk of heart attack or stroke.
- Other women who should not take the Pill are those who have had a heart attack, stroke, angina pectoris, blood clots, cancer of the breast or uterus. Women who have scanty or irregular periods should be encouraged to use some other method.
- A woman who believes she may be pregnant should not take the Pill because it increases the risk of defect in the foetus.
- Health problems such as migraine headaches, mental depression, fibroids of the uterus, heart or kidney disease, asthma, high blood pressure, diabetes or epilepsy may be made worse by use of the Pill.
- Risks associated with the Pill increase with age.

o

Long-Term Effect On Ability To Have Children.

- There is no evidence that using the Pill will prevent a woman from becoming pregnant after she stops taking it, although there may be delay before she is able to become pregnant. Women should wait a short time after stopping the Pill before becoming pregnant. During this time another method of contraception should be used.
- After childbirth the woman should consult her doctor before resuming use of the Pill. This is especially true for nursing mothers. The drugs in the Pill appear in the milk and the long-range effect on the infant is not known.

Intra-uterine Device (IUD). The IUD is a small plastic or metal device that is placed in the uterus (womb) through the cervical canal (opening into the uterus). As long as the IUD stays in place pregnancy is prevented. How the IUD prevents pregnancy is not completely understood. IUDs seem to interfere in some manner with implantation of the fertilised egg in the wall of the uterus. There are five kinds of IUDs currently available - Copper-7, Copper-T, Progestasert, Lippes Loop and Saf-T-Coil. IUDs containing copper (Copper-7 and Copper-T) should be replaced every three years. Those containing progesterone (Progestasert) should be replaced every year.

Effectiveness.

- Effectiveness depends on proper insertion by the doctor and whether the IUD remains in place.
- Of 100 women who use an IUD for one year, one to six will become pregnant.

Advantages.

- Once inserted by a doctor, no further care needed, except to see that the IUD remains in place (the user can check it herself but should be checked once a year by her doctor).

Disadvantages.

- May cause pain or discomfort when inserted. Afterwards may cause cramps and a heavier menstrual flow. Some women will experience adverse effects that require removal of the IUD.

- The IUD can be expelled, sometimes without being aware of it, leaving you unprotected.

Side Effects.
- Major complications, which are infrequent, include anaemia, pregnancy outside the uterus, pelvic infection, perforation of the uterus or cervix and septic abortion.
- A woman with heavy or irregular bleeding while using an IUD should consult her doctor. Removal of the IUD may be necessary to prevent anaemia.
- Women susceptible to pelvic infection are more prone to infection when using an IUD.
- Serious complications can occur if a woman becomes pregnant while using an IUD. Though rare, cases of blood poisoning, miscarriage and even death have been reported. An IUD user who believes she may be pregnant should consult her doctor immediately. If pregnancy is confirmed, the IUD should be removed.
- Although it rarely happens, the IUD can pierce the wall of the uterus when it is being inserted. Surgery is required to remove it.

Health Factors to Consider.
- Before having an IUD inserted, you should tell your doctor of any of the following: cancer or other abnormalities of the uterus or cervix; bleeding between periods or heavy menstrual flow; infection of the uterus, cervix, or pelvis (pus in fallopian tubes); prior IUD use; recent pregnancy, abortion, or miscarriage; uterine surgery; venereal disease; severe menstrual cramps; allergy to copper; anaemia; fainting attacks; unexplained genital bleeding or vaginal discharge; suspicious or abnormal smear test results.

Long-Term Effect On Having Children.
- Pelvic infection in some IUD users may result in their future inability to have children.

Diaphragm (With Cream, Jelly Or Foam). A diaphragm is a shallow cup of thin rubber stretched over a flexible ring. A sperm-killing cream or jelly is put on both sides of the diaphragm, which is then placed inside the vagina

51

before intercourse. The device covers the opening of the uterus, thus preventing the sperm from entering the uterus.

Effectiveness.
- Effectiveness depends on how correctly the method is used. Of 100 women who use the diaphragm with a spermicidal product for one year, 2 to 20 will become pregnant.

Advantages.
- No routine schedule to be kept as with the Pill. The diaphragm with a spermicidal product is inserted by the user.
- No discomfort or cramping, as with the IUD. No effect on the chemical or physical processes of the body, as with the Pill or the IUD.

Disadvantages.
- Must be inserted before each intercourse and stay in place 6 to 8 hours afterwards.
- Size and fit require yearly check-up and should be checked if you gain or lose weight.
- Should be refitted after childbirth or abortion.
- Requires instruction on insertion technique. Some women find it difficult to insert and inconvenient to use.
- Some women having a greatly relaxed vagina or "fallen" uterus cannot use a diaphragm successfully.

Side Effects.
- No serious side effects.
- Possible allergic reaction to the rubber or the spermicidal jelly. Condition easily corrected.

Foam, Cream Or Jelly Alone (Including Suppositories). Several brands of vaginal foam, cream or jelly can be used without a diaphragm. They form a chemical barrier at the opening of the uterus that prevents sperm from reaching an egg in the uterus. They also destroy sperm.

Effectiveness.
- Effectiveness depends on how correctly the method is used. Of 100 women who use aerosol foams alone for one year, 2 to 29 will become pregnant.
- Of 100 women who use jellies and creams alone for one year, 4 to 36 will become pregnant.
- No figures available for suppositories - considered fair to poor.

Advantages.
- Easy to obtain and use. No devices needed.

Disadvantages.
- Must be used one hour or less before intercourse. If placed earlier, may become ineffective.
- If douching is desired, must wait 6 to 8 hours after intercourse.

Side Effects.
- No serious side effects. Burning or irritation of the vagina or penis may occur. Allergic reaction may be corrected by changing brands.

Female Sterilisation. The primary method of sterilisation for women is tubal sterilisation, commonly referred to as "tying the tubes". A surgeon cuts, ties or seals the fallopian tubes to prevent passage of eggs between the ovaries and the uterus. Several techniques are available. With one new technique, the operation can be performed in a hospital out-patient surgical clinic with either a local or general anaesthetic. Using this method, the doctor makes a tiny incision in the abdomen or vagina and blocks the tubes by cutting, sealing with an electric current, or applying a small band or clip. Hysterectomy, a surgical procedure involving removal of all or part of the uterus, obviously prevents pregnancy, but is performed for other medical reasons and is not considered primarily a method of sterilisation.

Effectiveness.
- Virtually 100%.

Advantages.
- A one-time procedure - never any more bother with devices or preparations of any kind.

Disadvantages.

- Surgery is required. Although in some cases a sterilisation procedure has been reversed through surgery, the procedure should be considered permanent.

Side Effects.

- As with any surgery, occasionally there are complications, such as severe bleeding, infection or injury to other organs which may require additional surgery to correct.

Health Factors to Consider.

- There is some risk associated with any surgical procedure, which varies with the general health of the patient.

Long-Term Effect On Ability To Have Children.

- When the traditional type of tubal ligation is used, it is reversible in some cases. However, ability to reverse should not be counted on.

Male Sterilisation. Sterilisation of men involves severing the tubes through which the sperm travel to become part of the semen. The man continues to produce sperm but they are absorbed by the body rather than being released into the semen. This operation, called a vasectomy, takes about half an hour and may be performed under local anaesthetic. A vasectomy does not affect a man's physical ability to have intercourse.

Effectiveness.

- Virtually 100%.

Advantages.

- A one-time procedure that permits the man to resume normal activity almost immediately.

Disadvantages.

- The man is not sterile immediately after the operation - usually it takes a few months. Other means of contraception must be used during that time.

Side Effects.

- Complications occur in 2 to 4% of cases, including infection, haematoma (trapped mass of clotted blood), granuloma (an inflammatory reaction to sperm that is absorbed by the body), and swelling and tenderness near the testes. Most such complications are minor and are treatable without surgery.
- Studies by the National Institutes of Health show that vasectomy does not affect a man's sexual desire or ability.

Long-Term Effect on Ability to Have Children.

- Male sterilisation is reversible in a fair number of cases but ability to reverse should not be counted on.

Condom. The condom is a thin sheath of rubber that fits over the penis.

Effectiveness.

- Effectiveness depends on how correctly the method is used. Of 100 women whose partner uses a condom for one year 3 to 36 women will become pregnant.

Advantages.

- In addition to contraception, may provide some protection against venereal disease and AIDS.
- Easily available. Requires no "long-term" planning before intercourse.

Disadvantages.

- Some people feel the condom reduces pleasure in the sex act.
- The male must interrupt foreplay and fit the condom in place before sexual entry into the woman.
- The condom can slip or tear during use or spill during removal from the vagina.

Side Effects.

- No serious side effects. Occasionally an individual will be allergic to the rubber, causing burning, irritation, itching, rash or swelling, but this can easily be treated. Switching to a natural skin condom may be a solution.

Natural Family Planning (Rhythm Method). The woman must refrain from sexual intercourse on days surrounding the predicted time of monthly ovulation or, for greater effectiveness, until a few days after the predicted time of ovulation. Ways to determine the approximate time of ovulation include a calendar method, temperature method, cervical mucus method and a sympto-thermal method. Using the calendar method requires careful record-keeping of the time of the menstrual period and calculation of the time in the month when the woman is fertile and must not have intercourse. To use the temperature method, the woman must use a special type of thermometer and keep an accurate daily record of her body temperature (body temperature rises after ovulation). To use the cervical mucus method the woman must keep an accurate daily record of the type of vaginal secretions present. To use the sympto-thermal method the woman must observe the changes in her cervix, cervical mucus, and also record her body temperature every day to pinpoint her fertile period. The temperature method, mucus method, or sympto-thermal method used alone or concurrently with the calendar method are more effective than the calendar method alone.

Effectiveness.
- Effectiveness depends on how correctly the method is used. Of 100 women who use the calendar method for one year, 14 to 47 will become pregnant.
- Of 100 women who use the temperature method for one year, 1 to 20 will become pregnant.
- Of 100 women who use the mucus method for one year, 1 to 25 will become pregnant.
- Of 100 women who use, for one year, the temperature or mucus method with intercourse only after ovulation, less than 1 to 7 will become pregnant.
- Of 100 women who use the symptom-thermal method for one year, 1 to 22 will become pregnant.

Advantages.
- No drugs or devices needed.

Disadvantages.
- Requires careful record-keeping and estimation of the time each month when there can be no intercourse.

- To use any of the three methods properly a doctor's guidance may be needed, at least at the outset.
- If menstrual cycles are irregular, it is especially difficult to use this method effectively.
- Dissatisfaction because of extended time each month when sexual intercourse must be avoided.

Side Effects.
- No physical side effects, but because the couples must refrain from having intercourse except on certain days of the month, using this method can create pressures on the couple's relationship.

Withdrawal (Coitus Interruptus). This method of contraception requires withdrawal of the penis from the vagina before the man ejaculates, so the male sperm are not deposited at or near the birth canal. This method should not be considered effective for preventing pregnancy.

Douching. Use of a vaginal douche immediately after sexual intercourse to wash out or inactivate male sperm is not considered effective for preventing pregnancy.

COOLING DOWN IN HOT WEATHER

Follow These Simple Tips.
- Reduce calorie intake. Eat less fats and proteins. Eat more carbohydrates such as vegetables and fruits.
- Avoid midday sun.
- Wear light clothing. Light colours are good because they reflect sun. Dark clothing absorbs the sun.
- Drink at least eight glasses of liquid a day. Water is the best drink. Take time out to drink liquids even if you don't feel thirsty.
- Eating melons is a good way to increase your fluid intake. Water-melons and cantaloups contain a significant amount of water.
- Make sure drinks do not have sugar in them.
- Eat small meals rather than large ones. Digestion adds to body heat.
- Replace potassium and salt lost through sweat. Citrus fruit and bananas are good sources of potassium.

- Avoid alcoholic beverages. They act as a diuretic resulting in faster water loss.
- Take cool showers. Water removes extra body heat 25 times faster than cool air.
- Avoid heavy physical activity.

If Body Temperature Reaches 105 Degrees Fahrenheit (Heat Stroke).
1. Spray victim with hose. Sponge bare skin with cold water or rubbing alcohol. Apply cold packs to the victim's body.
2. Continue treatment until body temperature is lowered to 101 - 102 degrees Fahrenheit.
3. Do not over chill. Check temperature constantly.
4. Dry victim off once temperature is lowered.
5. Seek medical attention quickly.

COSMETICS

Little Difference Among Brands. Most cosmetics on the market today have similar ingredients, according to reports by the US Food and Drug Administration. This means that expensive products are no more effective than moderately priced ones. With the expensive face cream, the buyer may be paying for an attractive jar or a brand name.

CRABS

What To Do. Crabs are tiny insects that infest the pubic hair area. They attach to the base of the hair root. They cause blue spots on the skin and considerable itching.

Crabs can be transmitted through personal contact or sexual intercourse. They can also be acquired from a toilet seat, clothing or sleeping in an infested bed.

Treatment consists of rubbing the affected area with an anti-crab ointment available from your doctor.

DANDRUFF

Controlling Dandruff. Dandruff is a mild inflammation of the scalp causing flaking. These flakes are often highly visible on the hair and even fall on to the shoulders. A compound called selenium, found in several shampoo products, is highly effective in controlling dandruff. The shampoo should be left on at least five minutes before rinsing thoroughly. The hair and scalp should be shampooed at least once a week.

Vitamins And Minerals. Richard Gerson, PhD, in his book "The Right Vitamins", says dandruff may be due to nutritional deficiencies. He recommends getting adequate amounts of vitamin B-6, B-12, F and selenium in your diet.

Peanut Oil And Lemon. Many people report relief from dandruff with an old-time remedy combining peanut oil and lemon juice. Simply rub warm peanut oil into your scalp. Then apply the juice from a fresh lemon. Leave on for a few minutes then shampoo your hair. According to Dr Alan Shalita of the State University of New York Dermatology Department, the old-time remedy has value.

DENTURES

Calcium Helps Living With Dentures. Dentures can often be inconvenient, clumsy and cause considerable pain. A large part of the discomfort of dentures can come from the underlying bone in the gums which shrinks and causes improper fit.

Adding extra calcium to your diet can slow down the bone shrinking process, says Dr Kenneth Wycal from Loma Linda University. Dr Wycal studied two groups of denture wearers. One group supplemented their diets with 750 mg of calcium plus vitamin D each day. The other group did not supplement their diet. After one year those supplementing their diets with calcium and vitamin D lost an average of 34% less jawbone than the others, making dentures fit better. Foods rich in vitamin D include milk, salmon, tuna and sardines.

DEPRESSION (THE BLUES)

Chasing Away The Blues. Depression might last for days, weeks or even longer. Women suffer from depression twice as often as men. Many experts believe depression often stems from anger that is not expressed. These held-in feelings eventually turn into depression. If depression continues professional help may be needed. The following suggestions may help beat the blues:

- *Minerals May Help.* Calcium and magnesium may help the blues, according to one study published in the Journal of Nervous and Mental Disease. The study showed that depressed patients had significantly lower blood levels of magnesium than healthy people.

  Dr August Daro, a Chicago obstetrician and gynaecologist, says he routinely gives his depressed patients calcium and magnesium. He recommends combinations of 400 mg of calcium and 200 mg of magnesium per day. These minerals calm the nervous system and make depressed people feel better. He also recommends calcium and magnesium for premenstrual depression. Calcium and magnesium are available at most chemists and health food shops.
- *Low Folic Acid and Depression.* Researchers found that folic acid levels were significantly lower in depressed patients than in patients not suffering from depression, according to a study published in Psychosomatics. Folic acid is part of the vitamin B family. It is crucial to the normal functioning of the central nervous system. Folic acid is available in most health food stores. Foods rich in folic acid include beets, cabbage, green leafy vegetables, citrus fruits and whole grains.
- *Amino Acid Tyrosine.* A study published in the American Journal of Psychiatry indicated that supplementing the diet with the amino acid tyrosine helped some patients with depression. Of the 11 patients included in the study, nine showed improvement after taking tyrosine.
- *Low Blood Sugar.* Low blood sugar (hypoglycemia) is a common cause of depression, according to Dr August Daro. When he sees a depressed patient, the first thing he does is give a glucose tolerance test to measure blood sugar levels.

- *Coffee and Depression.* Some doctors believe drinking a lot of coffee can cause anxiety and even depression. Symptoms of anxiety may occur after drinking as few as two cups of coffee - about 250 mg of caffeine. Cola beverages supply about 40 mg per serving. A small chocolate bar, about 25 mg. It doesn't take much to reach the 250 mg level, researchers say.
- *Low Tryptophane Levels.* A study published in the British Medical Journal researched 18 women who suffered from depression. The researcher found that blood levels of tryptophane were low in all 18 women.
- *Vitamin B-6 and Depression.* Numerous studies have shown that women on the birth control pill may become depressed due to low levels of vitamin B-6. For example, in one study published in the Medical Journal Lancet, doctors measured the blood level of vitamin B-6 in 39 depressed women taking the birth control pill. They found 19 had a severe vitamin B-6 deficiency. When these women were given vitamin B-6, sixteen improved in mood. Foods rich in vitamin B-6 include bananas, cabbage, green leafy vegetables, whole grains and fish.

  Another study showed that 15 depressed, pregnant women had low blood levels of vitamin B-6. These women were not, of course, taking birth control pills. This study was published in the Acta Obstetricia et Gynecologica Scandinavica.
- *Another Amino Acid May Help.* Researchers found that depressed patients may benefit from an amino acid called phenylalanine, according to a study performed at Queen Charlotte's Maternity Hospital in London.

Help Yourself. It's easier than you think to change your mood, according to Los Angeles psychologist, Dr Harriet Braiker, in her book "Getting Up When You're Feeling Down". Here are her suggestions:

1. Take some exercise - walking, swimming, dancing and cycling all boost your energy.
2. Treat yourself - re-read your favourite book, buy fresh flowers, have a massage or facial.
3. Talk - and really listen - to people who are in high spirits.
4. Hug someone. The easiest way to get affection is to give it.
5. Recall happy moments. Look through old photographs or letters, and remember that bad times pass.
6. Laugh - watch a comedy film.

7. Indulge your senses - listen to music, visit a perfume counter, taste ice-cream, go to an art gallery, have a bath by candlelight.
8. Act as though you feel happy - it will help make it come true.

DIARRHOEA

3 Natural Remedies.

- *Yoghurt.* Many countries use yoghurt as a treatment for diarrhoea. The friendly bacteria in yoghurt called acidophilus tends to help normalise bowel functions. Yoghurt has an antibiotic effect, especially against Escherichia Coli, the main cause of traveller's diarrhoea.
- *Bran.* Bran helps normalise the bowel function. It helps relieve both constipation and diarrhoea. Bran thickens the loose stool of diarrhoea and softens the hard, dry stools in constipation.
- *Carob Powder.* A Canadian study showed that 227 of 230 infants given carob powder in their formula milk got relief from diarrhoea. Only 3 cases were not helped. Carob contains a high level of fibre.

What To Eat.
1. Avoid solid foods.
2. Start a clear liquid diet to replace lost fluids. This would include water, tea, carbonated beverages, jelly or broth.
3. If diarrhoea lasts longer than a day or two, seek medical attention. Prolonged diarrhoea causes dehydration.

DIETING

How To Lose Weight Successfully. The cause of being overweight is nearly always the direct result of eating more food than is burned off by activity. These excess calories are stored in the body as fat. The more calories taken in above what is burned off, the fatter we become. Each 3,500 excess calories equals 1 pound of body fat.

The only way to lose weight is: eat less and exercise more. Low calorie eating habits that are nutritionally well-balanced are the key to successful weight loss. This, combined with a regular exercise programme, should keep weight off permanently. Anyone starting a diet and exercise programme should consult a doctor.

Dangers Of Obesity.

Being overweight exposes you to numerous risks and even premature death. Overweight persons are more prone to heart and kidney disease, diabetes, high blood pressure, liver disorders and arthritis. Being 20 lb overweight between the ages of 40 and 50 increases the chance of death 18%.

Avoid Crash Diets. Crash diets can be dangerous. Losing weight too fast may damage the heart, gastrointestinal trace and metabolism. Rigid dieting and extreme weight fluctuations increase risk of gall-stones, according to medical studies.

A study conducted at Case Western University showed that the most successful dieters lost weight at a slow, steady pace.

What To Do Before Meals.

- Don't let yourself get too hungry before meals.
- Tighten your belt.
- Eat a salad 10 or 15 minutes before your meal. This will help cut your appetite down. Of course, eat your salad with a low-calorie dressing.
- Drink a glass of iced water. It has a shrinking effect on the stomach, helps curb appetite and makes the stomach feel fuller, according to Dr Richard Hansen of Poland Spring Health Institute in Maine.
- Drink a large glass of water before each meal. Drink it slowly. Food is more than 50% water. When you crave food you may really be craving water.
- Drink a glass of fruit juice or eat a piece of fruit 30 to 45 minutes before a meal. The sugar in the fruit satisfies your craving for calories, so that you eat less in the meal, according to a study carried out at Yale University.
- Start a meal with a cup of low-calorie soup.

During Meals - Suggestions For Successful Dieting.

- Eat meals at regular intervals.
- Eat less sugar. Substitute artificial sweeteners instead.
- Cut down on alcohol intake. Whisky and beer are high in calories.
- Eat more fibre. Vegetables, fruit, whole grains and beans add bulk to your diet and make you feel full and satisfied.

- Cut down on fats. Don't fry your foods. Avoid fatty cuts of meat. Trim off all visible fat on your foods. Remove skin from chicken before cooking.
- Eat slowly. People who eat fast often overeat. This is because they eat so fast they don't realise how much they have eaten until it is too late. Try eating with a small cocktail fork.
- Instead of giving up your favourite food just eat those foods in much smaller quantities.
- Use herbs and spices to flavour food. Avoid high-calorie dressings and toppings.
- Take smaller bites and put your fork down after each bite. Put your meals on a small plate rather than a large plate.

Stopping The Binging Urge. When you get the urge to binge put on some of your tight clothes. Experience the discomfort for a few hours. Imagine how good it would feel to wear them without the tightness.
- To satisfy the snack cravings make ice lollies using a diluted fruit drink.
- When eating at a buffet or party with a wide variety of foods take only tiny servings of each dish.

Try Glucomannan Capsules. Preliminary research shows that taking glucomannan capsules before meals increases weight loss. Glucomannan capsules are available in health food shops. Glucomannan is a natural fibre that swells up in the stomach reducing the desire for food.

- A study conducted at Harvard showed that dieters lost twice as much weight on glucomannan capsules. One hundred overweight women were put on a 12 week diet of 1,000 calories a day along with 20 overweight men who consumed 1,200 calories a day. Ten minutes before each meal all dieters took 3 g of glucomannan in capsule form. After 12 weeks the dieters had lost an average of 15 pounds. That is more than double the average 7 pounds weight loss produced on similar diets without taking glucomannan capsules, the study showed.
- A study by the US Department of Agriculture suggests that women who are iron deficient don't burn fat as well as those who have enough iron in their blood. This means that for those lacking iron, exercising may not be as effective as it would normally be in helping them to lose weight. This can be remedied by eating more foods with high iron content, such as lean

red meat, cabbage, oatmeal and dark meat poultry. However, you should first have your blood tested by your doctor, as too much iron can be harmful.

Reading Labels For A Successful Diet. For a successful diet you should read product labels. Labels must list ingredients based on the quantity of each ingredient in descending order. If sugar is the first ingredient listed, that means there is more sugar in the product than any other ingredient. Products high in sugar and salt could hamper your diet efforts.

- Labels can call sugar something else. For example, sugar can also be called sucrose, glucose, dextrose, fructose, corn syrups, corn sweeteners and invert sugar.
- Labels may call salt something else. Names such as sodium benzoate, disodium phosphate and sodium propionate are actually names for salt.

Avoid Diet Drinks - May Cause Weight Gain. Artificial sweeteners put in diet drinks can make you gain weight, says Dr Dennis Remington, Director of the Eating Disorder clinic at Brigham-Young University. Here's why:

- Artifical sweeteners are many times sweeter than sugar so they cause a craving for sweets.
- To satisfy this craving for sweets, the person is more likely to eat chocolate or other sugary snacks.
- The sweetness of the diet drink actually fools your system into thinking your body has ingested sugar. As a result your body releases extra insulin that can lead to weight gain.

Reducing Desire For Sweets. A study published in Federation Proceedings showed that zinc can improve the ability to taste. Women showed a significant increase in the ability to taste sweetness. Getting adequate zinc in your diet may be one way to cut back your intake of sugar - and take in fewer calories.

Satisfying Cravings For Snacks. Snacking is one of the greatest enemies of a dieter. You must substitute low-calorie, nutritious foods for high-calorie, junk foods for a successful diet. Be prepared by having nutritious, low-calorie foods ready. The following foods are good to snack on while dieting:

- Fresh fruit such as apples, bananas, blue berries, cherries, grapes, peaches, plums and strawberries.
- Rye crackers with low-fat cheese, skinned chicken or turkey.
- Popcorn without butter.
- Low-fat vanilla yoghurt.
- Peanuts in the shell.
- Dry, unsweetened cereal.
- Peanut butter and celery.
- Smoothies (banana or one-half cup of strawberries blended with one cup of skimmed milk).
- Biscuits with reduced sugar and whole-wheat flour.
- Bran muffins.
- Artificially-sweetened gelatin.
- Raw vegetables such as cauliflower, cherry tomatoes, cucumbers, mushrooms and carrot sticks.

Other Suggestions.
- Brush teeth and tongue after meals. This will discourage snacking.
- Fill up on water when you start to feel hungry.

DIGESTION

Two Common Foods That Aid Digestion.   Drinking one ounce of pineapple juice mixed with one ounce papaya juice with each meal is a great way to aid digestion, according to Dr L L Schneider. Papaya contains the enzyme papain and pineapple the enzyme bromelain. Both enzymes promote digestion and combat excess stomach acid.

Papaya Tablets.   Many persons report that papaya tablets taken alone aid digestion. Even the US Department of Agriculture has praised the digestive aid value of papaya. Papaya tablets are available at health food shops.

DOG BITES

How To Prevent. When you're confronted with a hostile dog there are several precautions you should take to avoid being bitten.

- Never run, even if the dog rushes at you. This brings out the "chase instinct" in the dog.
- Don't show fear. It makes the dog think you are vulnerable.
- Never look a dog or any other threatening animal directly in the eye. This may lead the animal to believe he is being challenged.
- If possible, place something between you and the dog, like a package or a bag.
- Do not turn your back on the dog. Instead, turn your body sideways and back away very slowly.
- Do not try to make friends with the dog. Don't try to pet it and don't put your hands or face near it.
- If the dog does bite you, don't pull way. This will cause a tear and a worse wound.
- A dog that holds its tail high and stiff and its ears up showing its teeth can be very dangerous. Conversely, a dog whose tail is down and ears back is more likely to calm down when you freeze.

DRINKING (See Also ALCOHOL)

Causes Loss Of Vitamins. Drinking alcohol can destroy essential vitamins in your body. The three most important vitamins lost are thiamine, zinc and magnesium. Other vitamins lost through drinks are vitamin A, B-6, B-12, C, D, folic acid, riboflavin and calcium. If you drink more than two or three drinks a day consider supplementing your diet.

DRIVING

Reducing Driving Stress. Driving in rush-hour traffic can be one of the most stressful things in life. Here are some tips to avoid stress while driving.

- Breathe deeply. Listen to soothing music. Think about things you need to do.

- Get comfortable. Adjust your seat so you can see 10 ft ahead. Keep your knees slightly lower than your thighs.
- Once out of the car take a short walk. Stretch your legs and cool off, says the Stress Management Centre, Washington DC.

Driving Long Distances. It's a good idea to take periodic breaks. Research shows it's good to have a snack while on a break. Eating a snack seems to improve driving performance and cuts down on fatigue.

DROWSINESS

4 Tips To Help Stay Awake. When you get drowsy at the wrong time and cannot get a cup of coffee or do something else to revive yourself, here are four tips that may help keep you awake:

- Press your knees together or press your elbows against the arms of your chair. The physical exertion will increase your blood circulation and make you more alert.
- Pinch the inside of your mouth between your teeth hard enough to jolt you out of drowsiness.
- Tickle the roof of your mouth with the tip of your tongue.
- Say something, even whispering to yourself. Speaking stimulates the brain and awakens you.

DRY MOUTH

5 Tips May Help. Dry mouth is characterised by a significant decrease in saliva flow due to emotional stress, medication and dehydration. Doctors suggest the following to reduce discomfort:

- Drink more water and other fluids, except acidic juices and alcohol.
- Carry water with you if possible.
- Stop smoking.
- Avoid eating dry or coarse foods, but keep a sound diet.
- Avoid commercial mouthwashes.

DRY SKIN

3 Tips To Relieve.
- The best way to moisturise skin is to soak in water then pat skin dry.
- Rub oil on the skin after the bath to seal in moisture.
- Avoid strong deodorant soaps. They tend to aggravate dry skin. Use soaps containing cold cream.

DUSTBINS, CLEANING

How To Clean. Dustbins can be a source of bacteria and disease. They should be cleaned regularly. Wash them with a borax solution, then sprinkle some dry borax on the bottom.

EAR CARE

Keeping Ears Healthy.
- Do not regularly clean your ears - they clean themselves.
- Avoid loud noises such as rock concerts and gun shots. They can permanently damage nerves and cause irreversible hearing loss. Wear ear plugs when exposed to loud noises.

Itching Ears. Shampoos and hair sprays have ingredients that can make the inside of ears itch. Harsh ingredients can even irritate the ear canal.

How To Prevent Itching Ears.
- When showering or shampooing your hair, plug your ears with cotton wool. Apply some vaseline to the cotton wool to create a water-proof seal.
- After swimming make sure water doesn't lodge in your ear canal. To prevent, use an eye dropper to place a few drops of baby oil in each ear canal. Let sit for about a minute. Then drain out by tilting your head to the side.
- Itching is often caused by ear wax accumulation. Never use any sharp objects (like a cotton wool bud or pencil) to remove it. You could push the ear wax deeper into the ear drum.

Helping Itching Caused By Ear Wax. Rinse the ear canal with a rubber syringe filled with a 50/50 solution of white vinegar and water. Let the solution remain in the canal for two minutes. Then drain by tilting your head over a sink for two minutes. Repeat once every two weeks.

ECZEMA

Creams To Soothe. Eczema is an inflammation of the skin marked by itching, blistering, scaling and sometimes an oozing of fluid. About a third of all visits to a dermatologist are for some form of eczema. Most experts believe eczema is caused by an allergy to substances in the environment. Eczema is usually worse in the winter and improves in the summer.

Apply hydrocortisone cream. If not available, any cream for irritated skin can be used.

ELECTRIC SHOCK

What To Do If Someone Is Suffering Electric Shock. Be very careful - there is a risk of electrocution to the person trying to help. Don't touch the victim directly until the current is shut off or the person is no longer in contact with the electricity. Victims struck by lightning, of course, may be touched immediately.

Removing The Victim From The Source Of Electricity.
- Turn off the current. Remove the fuse or pull the main switch if possible. If not possible call the electric company to cut off electricity.
- To remove the victim from a live wire, stand on something dry such as a newspaper, board, blanket, rubber mat or cloth. Wear dry gloves if possible. Be extremely careful.
- Push the victim away from live wire with a dry board, stick or broom handle, or pull the victim away with a dry rope looped around an arm or leg. Never use anything metallic, wet or damp. Be careful. Do not touch the victim until free from the wire.

EMOTIONS

How To Control Your Emotions. The kind of expression you put on your face helps determine how you feel inside, says Dr Paul Ekman, Professor at the University of California, San Francisco. Research showed that by coaching students to move facial muscles a certain way their bodies also experienced like emotions of fear, anger, disgust and amusement. For example, a facial expression of fear caused the body to feel fear. Anger caused the body to feel anger. Sadness caused feelings of sadness.

Preliminary research also shows that a person can control the results of a lie detector test by the expressions put on his face. Russians train agents to be able to control the results of lie detector tests. The Russians have done more research in this area than the US.

ENERGY

How To Get More Energy.
- One of the best ways to get quick energy is by drinking a glass of grape juice, according to Dr L L Schneider in his book "Old-Fashioned Health Remedies". Grape juice is one of the most readily assimilated foods for quick energy.
- Taking in oxygen is another good way to get quick energy. The following walking and breathing exercise is an effective way to get more oxygen.
  1. Walk at a normal pace.
  2. Inhale counting as you go.
  3. Exhale slowly taking twice as long as inhalation to count.
  This simple exercise energises the body by increasing oxygen levels.

EYES

Removing Minor Foreign Objects. To remove a minor foreign object such as an eye lash, speck or cinder (that is floating on an eye ball or inside the eye lid) carefully follow these suggestions.
  1. Do not rub the eyes.
  2. Wash hands with soap and water.

3. Gently pull upper eye lid down over lower eye lid and hold for a moment. This causes tears to flow which sometimes washes out the particle.
4. If the particle is not removed, fill eye dropper with warm water. Squeeze water over the eye to flush out particle. If eye dropper is not available hold head under gentle stream of water to flush out particle.
5. If still unsuccessful gently pull lower eye lid down. If foreign body can be seen on the side of the lower lid, carefully lift particle out with a moistened corner of clean handkerchief, cloth or facial tissue.
6. If speck is not visible on the lower lid check the inside of upper lid. This can be done by first holding the lashes of the upper eye lid and pulling downward. You must look downward during this entire procedure. While holding the eye lid down place a match or cotton wool bud horizontally across the outside of the lid and flip the eye lid backward over the stick. Carefully remove particle with moistened corner of handkerchief, cloth or facial tissue. If particle still remains cover the eye with a sterile or clean compress and seek medical attention. Never attempt to remove any particle that is sticking in the eye ball. Seek medical attention for such injuries.

3 Suggestions To Avoid Eye Strain While Watching TV.
- Don't have a lamp near the screen so it can cause glare.
- Stay at least 7 ft from your TV. Never sit so you have to look up at the screen.
- Be sure all lighting in the room comes from behind and does not reflect off the screen.

Avoiding Eye Strain At Work. Here are some relaxation techniques that will help prevent eye strain and fatigue:

- Close your eyes for 5 minutes every few hours.
- Rub your hands together for a few minutes to make them warm. Lean back in a chair and cup your palms over your eyes. The heat will relax your eyes. Look out of the window or down a hall. Relax and try to look as broadly as you can, taking in everything for about 1 minute. This also tends to relax your eyes.

- Hold a pencil at arm's length and pull it slowly towards your eyes until you see double. Repeat for 1 minute a day. This will help strengthen eye muscles.

FACIAL HAIR

Ways To Get Rid Of.
- *Waxing.* Waxing is probably the best method for removing large areas of hair. If done correctly it can remove the root so the hair will not grow back. Be sure to buy a high quality wax that does not get brittle.
- *Shaving.* Shaving is the most popular, temporary solution to hair on the face. Of course, the hair grows back quickly. Stubble may eventually become a problem.
- *Depilatory Creams.* These creams dissolve unwanted hair leaving the skin surface smooth. But, they can create skin irritations. When using for the first time, make a patch test, following the instructions on the packet. This will tell you whether you are allergic to the compound.
- *Electrolysis.* This is the only permanent solution to hair growth. Electrolysis destroys the hair root so it will not grow back. If done properly it is very effective. However, electrolysis can be painful and costly.
- *Bleaching.* Bleaching may be a good solution for small amounts of hair. Bleaching the hair makes it less visible. This method is preferred for certain types of hair on the face. Bleaching must be done regularly. When the hair grows, the colour returns.
- *Tweezing.* Tweezing is an effective way to remove hair but is also painful. Many people apply wrapped ice to the skin after tweezing to reduce swelling.

FALLS, PREVENTING

8 Tips For Preventing Falls. Accidents seldom just happen - many can be prevented. Safety is especially important for older persons.

- Illuminate all stairways and provide light switches at both the bottom and the top.
- Provide night lights or bedside remote-control light switches.

- Be sure both sides of stairways have sturdy handrails.
- Tack down carpeting on stairs and use non-skid treads.
- Remove throw rugs that tend to slide.
- Arrange furniture and other objects so they are not obstacles.
- Use grab bars on bathroom walls and non-skid mats or strips in the bath.
- Keep outdoor steps and paths in good repair.

FATIGUE

Alleviating Fatigue.   People visit doctors for fatigue more than any other symptom. Fatigue can be due to physical or psychological factors. Prolonged fatigue requires professional attention to determine the underlying causes.

Reducing Fatigue-Causing Conditions.
- *Noises.* Noises can add to stress and trigger fatigue. Find a quiet place to work and relax.
- *Privacy.* Lack of privacy contributes to stress and fatigue. Find a place away from people.
- *Tight Clothing.* Avoid clothing that is too small or too tight. It can restrict the blood vessels and contribute to fatigue. Women should avoid tight girdles and bras.
- *Prescription Drugs.* Fatigue can often be caused by an adverse reaction to prescription drugs. Ask your doctor or pharmacist about side effects of medications.
- *Sleeping Conditions.* A sagging or uncomfortable mattress can rob you of sleep and cause fatigue. Sleep on a firm, quality mattress.
- *Eye Strain.* Make sure your glasses fit well. Be sure you have the proper prescription for your glasses.

Anti-Fatigue Research For Consideration.
- *Magnesium.* A deficiency of magnesium is a common cause of fatigue, says Dr Ray C Wunderlick of St Petersburg, Florida. In a research study 200 men and women suffering from tiredness were given magnesium. In all but two cases, tiredness disappeared. This study appeared in the Second International Symposium of Magnesium. Foods rich in magnesium include brown rice, bran, green vegetables, honey and seafood.

- *B-Vitamins.* One of the main reasons for chronic fatigue and tiredness is lack of B-vitamins, says Dr Lendon Smith, a nationally-known nutritional expert. A 25 mg daily does of B-complex is sufficient for most people to combat a deficiency. This amount of B-complex should increase energy levels and help you deal with stress better.

  One reason for a deficiency is the processing that foods go through. B-vitamins are some of the first to disappear when food is over-processed. Foods rich in B-complex vitamins include brewer's yeast germ, whole grains and yoghurt.

- *Potassium.* Potassium deficiency may be a cause of fatigue, especially in professional athletes and long-distance runners. This mineral helps cool muscles. Potassium is sometimes used up after hours of exertion or exercise. If it's not replaced, chronic fatigue may result. Foods rich in potassium include apricots, broccoli, peaches, dates, figs and seafood.

- *Vitamin B-6.* A study in the International Journal of Vitamin and Mineral Research showed that elderly patients in nursing homes are often deficient in the vitamin. The study showed that 56.6% of the patients in nursing homes were deficient in vitamin B-6. A deficiency of vitamin B-6 can cause fatigue. Foods rich in vitamin B-6 include bananas, cabbage, green leafy vegetables, whole grains and fish.

- *Wheat Germ Oil.* Wheat germ oil aids in the production of energy, says Dr Thomas K Cureton, Director of the Physical Fitness Institute at the University of Illinois. He has studied the effects of wheat germ oil for over 22 years. Wheat germ oil can increase energy, vitality and stamina. Wheat germ oil does not work overnight, says Dr Cureton. It takes about four to five weeks to feel a difference. About a teaspoonful a day will do. The oil is best absorbed when taken on a relatively empty stomach after exercise. Wheat germ oil is available at most health food shops.

- *Vitamin C.* Vitamin C and iron deficiencies may contribute to fatigue. Persons who received 1,000 mg of vitamin C a day reported less fatigue and faster reaction times, according to a study in the Review of Czechoslovak Medicine.

  Another study published in the Journal of the American Geriatrics Society surveyed 400 people about vitamin C intake and fatigue symptoms. The study showed those who took over 400 mg of vitamin C a day had less fatigue. Foods rich in vitamin C include citrus fruits and fruit juices, berries, cabbage, green vegetables and potatoes.

Other Factors Contributing To Fatigue.
- Drinking too much coffee or alcohol.
- Boredom. Lack of specific interest or ambition.
- Stress. Your body uses energy fighting stress. Things that cause stress include money worries, family conflicts and setting unrealistic goals for yourself.
- Lack of regular exercise can also contribute to stress. Even exercising 20 minutes a day, three times a week will help reduce stress.

FEARS

Things Men Fear Most. The five worst fears of men according to Dr William Appleton of Harvard and Dr Harvey L Ruben of Yale are:
- Fear of being fired. Most men base their self esteem on how well they do in their job.
- Fear of loss of health. Men fear being helpless and dependent on someone else.
- Fear of loss of physical power - especially sexual prowess.
- Fear of rejection by a loved one. Men have a fear of being abandoned.
- Fear their children will become failures. Men fear their children will be a burden on them later in life.

FEET

General Care Of Feet. Most important in foot care is properly fitting shoes. Never buy shoes that need breaking in. It's normally your feet that break in, not the shoes. Shoes should have rounded toes. High heels should be avoided. Rubber heels are better - they reduce shock on your feet. Shoes should be made of leather or canvas. The following tips will help you avoid problems:

- Wash feet daily. Rinse off all soap. Dry thoroughly, especially between toes.
- Trim nails straight across and not too short. Rounding off corners can lead to ingrown toe-nails. It is all right to file the corners a little to prevent ladders in stockings.

- Wear clean socks. Change daily.
- Switch shoes from day to day.
- Use foot powder.

Caring For Feet - Summer. Summer heat can make your feet swell up. This makes feet more susceptible to athlete's foot fungus. Foot experts recommend the following for hot weather foot care:

- Summer heat can make blood vessels dilate causing ankles to swell up. To prevent, take the weight off your feet by sitting down and raising feet off the ground. Flex your toes to get the blood pumping.
- Keep moving. Don't stand too long in one place. Standing still causes the fluids to accumulate in your feet.
- Wear comfortable shoes that are well cushioned. Make sure they are adequately ventilated.
- Dry feet thoroughly after showering. Dry very carefully between the toes and spray with an anti-fungal spray to keep athlete's foot fungus away.
- Bathe your feet using a two step process: Put feet in hot water for 3 minutes, then put in cold water for 1 minute. Repeat this several times. This will open and close veins and improve circulation.
- Massage feet using circular motions. This will make your whole body feel good.

Getting Shoes To Fit Correctly.
- Buy shoes late in the day when your feet are the most swollen. If you buy them early they are likely to feel too tight a few hours later, says Dr Barry Block.
- Make sure the largest part of your foot matches the widest part of your shoe.
- There should be a half inch space between the end of your longest toe and the front of the shoe when standing up.
- Do not accept a different size from that which you normally wear.
- Buy shoes made from natural, breathable material such as leather.
- The back of the shoe where the heel goes in should be stiff.
- The shoe sole should be flexible near the ball of the foot and should bend easily.
- Soles should be made of a shock absorbent material such as crêpe.

- The maximum heel height for comfortable walking is 2 inches.

Prevent Odour From Shoes And Feet. Smelly feet are often caused by bacteria lodged in the shoes. You can keep your shoes and feet bacteria and odour free by following these tips:

- Always wear socks with shoes - cotton ones are best because they absorb moisture.
- Wear leather shoes because they allow perspiration to evaporate.
- Use an antiperspirant on the soles of your feet.
- Use an anti-bacterial foot powder, or, just as good, baking soda.
- Once a week air your shoes in the sunlight. Sunlight kills germs.
- The same shoes should not be worn two consecutive days.
- Spray your shoes with an anti-bacterial spray once a week. Allow them to dry out for a day.
- Insert an ultraviolet light in your shoes periodically. This will help kill bacteria.

FINGERNAILS

Identifying Health Problems In Fingernails.
- *Brittle Nails.* Brittle nails are a common problem in women. One reason may be iron deficiency. Researchers in Sheffield, England, found that nails are sensitive to iron shortages in the system. A shortage in iron can make the nails brittle. Foods rich in iron include dark green, leafy vegetables, fish, legumes and whole grains.
- *White Spots.* White spots on the nails may indicate zinc deficiency. Foods rich in zinc include seafood, spinach, mushrooms, whole grains and sunflower seeds.
- *Yellow Nails.* Yellow nails may indicate a shortage of vitamin E. They may also indicate problems in the lymph system or respiratory problems. Foods rich in vitamin E include dark green vegetables, fruits and rice.
- *White Nails.* White nails may indicate chronic anaemia or liver or kidney problems.

FIREPLACE

Danger Of Lead Poisoning. Do not burn any coloured newspapers or magazines in your fire place. Coloured newspapers contain lead. When this lead is burned it can emit dangerous levels of lead into your home. It is especially dangerous to children.

FIRES

Baking Soda For Kitchen Fires. It is a good idea to keep a box of baking soda near the cooker. This can be an ideal way to douse a fire. Never use water on a fire in the kitchen. This will make the fire worse in most cases.

Avoiding Kitchen Fires.
- Regularly inspect appliances for frayed cords or other malfunctions.
- If an appliance gets wet or is not working properly have it serviced immediately. Do not keep using it.
- Never overload a circuit. It can overheat and cause a fire.
- When replacing a fuse always use the same size. Never use a larger fuse that could cause the circuit to overheat.
- Do not store items you often need in a place where you have to lean over the cooker. When cooking do not wear clothing with loose sleeves that can catch fire on the burners.
- Keep pan handles turned in so your children can't pull them off the cooker and severely burn themselves.

FIRST AID

Suggested Items For Most Families. It is a good idea to have useful medical supplies on hand for emergencies and home treatment of minor ailments.

Drug Items.
- Analgesic-aspirin and/or paracetamol. Both reduce fever and relieve pain.
- Indigestion tablets.
- Antiseptic cream.
- Hydrocortisone creams for skin problems.

- Calamine for rashes and sunburn.
- Petroleum jelly for chapped skin, minor burns and scrapes.
- Anti-diarrhoea tablets.
- Cough syrup - non-suppressant type.
- Decongestant.

Non-Drug Items.
- Adhesive plasters of assorted sizes.
- Sterile gauze in pads and a roll.
- Absorbent cotton.
- Adhesive tape.
- Elastic bandage.
- Small, blunt-end scissors.
- Tweezers.
- Fever thermometer, including rectal type for a young child.
- Hot water bottle.
- Heating pad.
- Eye cup for flushing objects out of the eye.
- Ice bag.
- Dosage spoon (common household teaspoons are rarely the correct dosage size).
- Vaporiser or humidifier.
- First aid manual.

Other Important Suggestions.
- Keep all medicines out of reach of children.
- Medicines should have child resistant caps. Elderly persons who have difficulty opening such caps should ask their chemist for standard caps.
- Keep medicines in a cool, dry place away from food and other household products.
- Keep prescription and non-prescription drugs separated with clear labels.
- Check medicine chest supplies periodically. Get rid of spoiled or outdated products.
- Keep handy telephone numbers of your doctor's surgery, clinic and hospital and have this list near every telephone and inside the bathroom medicine cabinet door.

FLATTENING YOUR TUMMY

The 20-Second Miracle. A simple exercise to flatten your stomach takes just 20 seconds. You can do it anywhere.

- Sit upright or stand straight. Suck in your stomach holding it for approximately 20 seconds. Then let go.
- Don't hold your breath while doing the exercise. Just breathe normally.
- Repeat the exercise several times per day. You should aim for doing it approximately 16 times a day, according to Dr David Bachman.
- You should see results in a short time. Your abdomen will start to look flatter and feel tighter.

FLEAS

Keeping Your Pet Free Of Fleas. Fleas can affect humans in addition to dogs and cats. Fleas can burrow under the skin causing inflammation and itching. Fleas may also carry diseases such as typhus and bubonic plague. (This is rare with domestic pets.) These suggestions should help rid your pet of fleas:

- At least every other day vacuum the area where your pet sleeps.
- Add brewer's yeast tablets to your pet's diet. The vitamin B-1 in yeast is believed to emit an odour on skin that fleas hate.
- Wash your pet's bedding at least once a week.
- Give your pet a bath and then rinse in the following solution: Slice two lemons including the peel, and place in 2 pints of boiling water for an hour. Let stand overnight. Strain the next morning and sponge solution on to your pet. The lemon scent repels fleas yet has a pleasant odour.

Keeping Your Home Free Of Fleas. It is important to minimise the number of fleas in your home. Your pet may be free of fleas, but whenever he enters your home the fleas will jump back on him. A simple procedure may be effective in ridding your home of fleas. Here is what to do:

- Place a shallow dish of soapy water on your carpet overnight. Place a small lamp beside it so the light shines directly on the water.
- Fleas are attracted to light. They will jump at it bouncing into the soapy water where they drown, according to Moira Anderson of Dog Fancy Magazine.
- The soap softens the water causing the fleas to sink once they hit it. If just plain water is used, the fleas will simply jump out again.
- It is necessary to follow this procedure for about a week. At first, you will catch a large number of fleas. Then the number will decrease. The number of fleas may increase a few days later as hatched eggs start to be attracted to the lamp.
- The rest of the room should be dark. Be sure to keep your pet out of the room so he does not disturb the bowl of water or the lamp.

FLU

What To Do When The Bug Strikes.
- Stay in bed if possible.
- Take aspirin or paracetamol. Do not take aspirin with vitamin C. It may increase stomach irritation. (For children consult your doctor before administering aspirin.)
- Avoid further complications by staying away from crowds.
- Drink plenty of liquids.
- Do not smoke. Cigarette smoking weakens resistance and lung power.
- Take vitamin C supplements (but not with aspirin). Eat properly and consult your doctor if your condition worsens.

FOOD ADDITIVES

May Be Harmful To Your Health. Health experts are becoming increasingly concerned over potential harmful effects of food additives. Some food additives have been linked to allergies and other reactions.

Here is a listing of common additives and their potential harmful effects.

- *Monosodium Glutamate (MSG).* This is a flavour enhancer. It can cause several reactions such as sleepiness, aching, sweating, headaches and other allergic reactions.
- *Brominated Vegetable Oil (BVO).* This is added to fruit flavoured soft drinks to keep the ingredients blended. BVO can build in body fat and may cause long term effects.
- *Methylcellulose.* This is a thickener used in beverages, tinned fruits and kosher foods. In some cases it may bring about allergies.
- *Talc.* It is used to dust chewing gum. Talc is also used as a filler in vitamin capsules. Talc may contain harmful asbestos fibre.
- *Butylated Hydrosytoluene (BHT).* This is a preservative used in many foods such as cereals and chewing gum. Studies indicate BHT may cause cancer.

FOOD POISONING

Tips For Preventing Poisoning. Food poisoning can be very serious. Symptoms include nausea, vomiting, diarrhoea and abdominal cramps. Medical attention should be sought if symptoms become severe or persist for more than 24 hours. Here are a few tips to avoid food poisoning.

- Keep hot foods hot and cold foods cold. Hot foods should be kept at 140 degrees or greater. Cold foods need to be stored at 45 degrees or less. Food kept between these temperatures is prone to rapid bacterial growth and resulting food poisoning.
- Bacteria in raw poultry, fish and meat can contaminate cutting boards. Scrub with bleach after use.
- Do not use tins of food that have bulged. Avoid unusual coloured food. If the food looks bad, never taste for spoilage. Even a tiny amount of bacteria can cause botulism that can be fatal.
- If you become ill after eating at a restaurant, immediately notify the restaurant owners. The local environmental health department should also be notified.

Suggestions For Avoiding Picnic Food Poisoning. Food poisoning is a greater risk in the warmer months because of the difficulty in transporting food at safe temperatures. Modern cool bags have made transportation to the picnic site easier, but there are several things you can do to minimise the risk of food poisoning.

- Keep the more perishable foods at the bottom of your cool bag. Heat rises. So the bottom is colder than the top.
- Before leaving for the picnic, freeze as many foods and drinks as possible. This will minimise bacterial contamination.
- Separately pack picnic items in plastic bags. If picnics include sandwiches, keep the ingredients separate until you reach the picnic site.
- It's better not to transport raw chicken to the picnic site. Cook at home and reheat when you get there. Be sure cooked chicken is kept below 45 degrees in transit.
- Ground meat is more perishable than solid pieces of meat and should be cooked first.
- Certain picnic foods are particularly prone to contamination. These include potato salad, egg and tuna salad. Be sure to keep them below 45 degrees.

Common Types Of Bacteria Causing Food Poisoning.

- *Salmonella.* Common in raw meat, poultry, milk and eggs. Flies, other insects and pets can carry this bacteria. There are 1,700 types of Salmonella bacteria. Symptoms develop within 8 to 72 hours of eating contaminated food. Symptoms may include diarrhoea, cramps, nausea and vomiting.
- *Staphylococci.* The most common bacteria causing food poisoning. Develops in meat, poultry, eggs, custards, cream-filled pastries, potato salads and many other foods. Most often caused by leaving foods to stand for too long at room temperature. Symptoms develop within 1 to 8 hours after eating contaminated foods. Symptoms include vomiting, cramps and diarrhoea.
- *Escherichia Coli.* This bacteria is the main cause of traveller's diarrhoea. It is often transported in the water supply because of sewage contamination. Symptoms occur within 8 to 44 hours after ingestion and include mild to severe diarrhoea.
- *Clostridium Botulinum.* This bacteria occurs in home-canned or any tinned goods showing signs of being dented or swollen. Symptoms develop in 12 to 48 hours and include double vision, trouble speaking and swallowing. Left untreated botulism can be fatal.

- *Raw Seafood.* Raw and undercooked fish and shellfish should be avoided because they may be contaminated by sewage. Play it safe by cooking all fish well; this will destroy any disease-producing bacteria.

FRECKLES

Sugar And Freckles. Eliminating refined sugar from your diet may keep freckles under control. The more refined sugar you have in your diet, the more likely you are to have dark freckles, according to William Dufty, author of "Sugar Blues".

FROST BITE

Damages Your Skin. Frost bite is damaging to the skin due to overexposure to cold weather. It usually affects parts of the body having the poorest circulation like the ears, hands, feet and face. People with impaired circulation or diabetes are particularly prone to frost bite.

Symptoms Of Frost Bite.
1. Skin appears red in the early stages. Pain is common.
2. As the frost bite develops, skin becomes greyish and appears waxy.
3. Ears feel cold and numb.
4. Pain disappears.
5. The skin may blister.

What To Do.
1. Do not rub ears with snow or anything else.
2. Bring victim inside promptly.
3. Gently wrap ears in warm material.
4. Do not use heat lamps, hot water bottles or heating pads.
5. Do not allow victim to place frost bitten ears near a hot stove or radiator.
6. Do not break blisters.
7. Seek medical attention promptly.

Avoiding Frost Bite.
- Wear footwear that is waterproof. Wear absorbent socks to help control perspiration.
- Be sure socks are the right size with ample room for toes. Socks should not restrict circulation. Avoid factors that contribute to frost bite, such as fatigue, alcohol use and smoking.
- Keep feet dry and warm. It is not cold alone that causes frost bite. Dampness also causes it. If feet get wet or damp, change to warm, dry footwear at once.
- In a very cold climate, supplementing the diet with about 425 mg a day of vitamin C helps maintain skin temperature. Foods rich in vitamin C include citrus fruits and fruit juices, berries, cabbage, green vegetables and potatoes.

GALL-STONES

Persons At Risk Of Gall-stones. Gall stones are hardened, stone-like masses mostly formed by cholesterol. They form in the gall-bladder area and cause inflammation and discomfort. Frequently, the pain develops suddenly after meals. With strong symptoms, surgery is normally warranted. A medication is now available that can dissolve the stones in some cases. Twice as many women as men develop gall-stones. The following people have an increased risk of gall-stones:

- Overweight persons who frequently lose weight then regain it.
- Women having two or more children.
- Those eating a high-fat diet and having high cholesterol blood levels.

Avoiding Gall-stones - Preliminary Research.
- *Fasting.* Long intervals between meals might increase the risk of gall-stones, according to a study published in a British medical journal. The length of time between dinner and breakfast is especially crucial. Those skipping breakfast or drinking only coffee are reported to be at greater risk of gall-stones.
- *Bran.* Adding bran to the diet may help provide some protection from gall-stones, says Dr D E W Pomare. According to a research study, those

adding bran to their diet every day significantly reduced cholesterol saturation in the bile. Cholesterol is the chief constituent of most gall-stones. Dr Pomare recommends complete unprocessed bran. The larger size of unprocessed bran is believed more effective than the smaller particles.

- *Lecithin.* According to a study published in the American Journal of Gastroenterology, eight patients suffering gall-stones were given lecithin. Lecithin reduced pain and altered bile chemistry in a way that would help dissolve the gall-stones. Lecithin is available in most health food shops. Granules are much more potent than capsules. A typical lecithin capsule is 1,200 mg, but one tablespoon of lecithin equals 10 typical capsules. Many people sprinkle lecithin granules on their cereals in the morning.

GOUT

Cherries May Help. Gout is a form of arthritis that is believed to be inherited. It's caused by faulty metabolism of protein which causes high levels of uric acid in the system. The uric acid forms crystals which lodge in the joints - mostly the big toe. This causes considerable pain. Typical victims are men in their early 40s. Women rarely suffer gout.

Some gout sufferers have reported that cherries relieve the pain from gout. They say that cherries - either tinned, fresh, frozen or even juice concentrate - eased their suffering.

GREY HAIR

One Doctor's Way To Prevent Grey Hair. According to Dr Abram Hoffer, a psychiatrist from Canada, taking an 800 IU capsule of vitamin E every day prevented his hair from going grey. The doctor brags of a healthy head of hair that is all black with no grey whatsoever. Dr Hoffer believes grey hair is a symptom of body degeneration and vitamin E helps halt this condition. Foods rich in vitamin E include dark green vegetables, fruit and rice.

GUM DISEASE

Preventing Gum Disease. About 75% of men and women over the age of 35 suffer from some periodontal (gum) disease, says the American Dental

Association. For people over 60 years old, almost 40% have lost teeth because of it. Gum disease starts when plaque forms on the teeth. Plaque is a sticky film of food and bacteria that accumulates between the teeth along the gum lines. If you don't remove the plaque every day it will attack your gums. With the first stages of gum disease, your gums become inflamed, may bleed and pull away from the teeth. With the second stage (pyorrhoea) of the disease, pus may ooze out of the gums. Pain may be extreme. Teeth eventually become loose and fall out. Gum disease is reversible if treated before it reaches the advanced stage. The following tips may help avoid gum disease.

- *Flossing.* Careful brushing and flossing at least two or three times a day is the best defence.
- *Cleaning.* It is important to have your teeth cleaned regularly by a professional. They can get to many areas where brushing and flossing cannot.
- *Vitamin C.* Preliminary research shows that vitamin C may help protect the gums against infection. A study published by the International Journal of Vitamin and Nutritional Research showed that volunteers given 70 mg of vitamin C a day for six weeks showed an improvement in gum disease.
- *Calcium.* Research has shown that calcium is also a key factor in the prevention and treatment of gum disease. A calcium deficiency can weaken the bones which house the teeth and make the body more susceptible to infections, says Dr Paul Keyes of the International Dental Foundation. Foods rich in calcium include low-fat milk, green leafy vegetables, legumes, salmon and low-fat yoghurt.

Home Prevention Method. Wet toothbrush in hydrogen peroxide or water. Dip the brush in baking soda and salt. Smear this mixture along the gum lines. Make sure all crevices between the gums and teeth are covered, then rinse thoroughly. This method kills the bacteria and foams it away, thus helping to prevent gum disease, according to the International Dental Foundation.

Get Second Opinion. A national magazine reported that many dentists specialising in gum disease (Periodontist) may prescribe unnecessary, often painful gum treatments. Reporters visited eight periodontists in locations across the United States. One half of the periodontists visited prescribed unnecessary gum treatment. Get a second opinion.

HAEMORRHOIDS

Suggestions For Haemorrhoid Relief. Haemorrhoids are swollen veins in the anus and anal area. Haemorrhoids in the anus area are called external. Anal haemorrhoids are called internal. About 35% of the population suffers from haemorrhoids.

Haemorrhoids cause itching, burning and sometimes bleeding. Flareups can be due to habitual postponement of bowel movement, constipation and straining. Diet plays a major role in haemorrhoids. A diet high in refined foods such as white flour and sugar increases chances of haemorrhoids. The following suggestions may help to avoid them:

- Eat bulky foods such as grains, leafy vegetables and fruits. This should help regulate bowel movements.
- Try warm water soaks to avoid discomfort.
- After bowel movements, pat yourself clean with a damp cloth. Avoid excess wiping with tissue paper.
- Drink plenty of liquids every day.
- Avoid lifting heavy objects.
- Use a stool softener if stool is excessively hard. Use a laxative if constipated to avoid straining. (Stool softeners and laxatives are available at chemists.)
- Never postpone a bowel movement. When nature calls, answer as soon as possible.

HAIR ANALYSIS

Unreliable Results. Some commercial laboratories analyse hair samples and report mineral content. This information is supposedly useful in determining what sort of mineral supplements a person should take. However, a report in the Journal of the American Medical Association says that it is not possible to correlate most hair mineral levels with your nutritional status. For example, hair levels of zinc may be normal or even high in people with a severe zinc deficiency. The article says that hair analysis is only useful in cases of suspected poisoning for substances like arsenic where the presence of massive amounts of the poison in the hair would be important in making a diagnosis of the problem.

- The article reports on sending 52 hair samples from two healthy people to 13 laboratories. The reports from these laboratories varied considerably for identical samples. Different results for the same hair were returned from the same laboratory. Some reports from these laboratories concluded that the individual needed mineral supplements. Some laboratories offered to sell supplements to the report recipients.

HAIR CARE

11 Hair Care Tips.
- Keep brushes and combs clean - they can irritate the scalp and inhibit hair growth.
- A scarf or hat will protect your hair from the sun and wind. Wear a cap to protect your hair from the chlorine in a swimming pool. Shampoo hair immediately after swimming.
- If your hair has been permed too tight, use a heavy duty protein conditioner.
- Some shampoos can cause flaking and scaling of the scalp. If this happens, change your shampoo.
- To avoid damaging hair when blow-drying, use a lotion or styling mousse. Don't keep the dryer too close to your hair. Don't hold it in one place too long. Keep the air moving throughout the hair.
- Split ends should be removed by cutting a quarter of an inch off your hair.
- To combat the frizzies, use a conditioner or hot oil treatment once a week.
- Hair static can be controlled with a very light hair spray, mist or water.
- Don't fight a natural wave.
- Normal hair loses between 30 and 100 hairs a day. Don't overbrush your hair. It may cause damage and contribute to hair loss.
- Never brush wet hair. Hair is very fragile when wet.

Removing Gum From Hair. To remove gum or tar from hair, rub with vegetable oil. Then wash with soap and water.

HANGOVERS

All Alcohol Not The Same. Hangovers are basically caused by manufacturing by-products in alcohol beverages called congeners, according to experiments performed at Columbia University College of Pharmaceutical Sciences in New York City. Researchers had volunteers drink an alcoholic beverage that had been poured through a charcoal filter to filter out congeners. Other volunteers drank the alcohol as it came out of the bottle. Researchers assessed hangover symptoms the next day. Those who drank the alcohol filtered through the charcoal had considerably less hangover symptoms.

Alcohol That Causes The Worst Hangovers. Whisky has a large amount of congeners. People who drink whisky are more likely to have severe hangovers, reported psychologist Dr Loring Chapman of the University of California at Davis.

Other alcohol drinks that give bad hangovers are brandy, rum, and red wine. All contain high amounts of congeners. Vodka and gin have the fewest congeners. They normally provide the least severe hangovers.

Getting Rid Of A Hangover. Sauerkraut juice mixed with tomato juice (in equal parts) is one of the best cures for a hangover, according to Dr L L Schneider, a practising physician.

Vitamin C. According to Dr Neil Solomon, vitamin C minimises the adverse effects of alcohol. A study showed vitamin C speeds up the exit of alcohol from the body and shortens the length of time of a hangover.

HEADACHE

Suggestions To Prevent Headache. Headaches are one of the most common reasons why people visit a doctor. Headache pain does not originate in the brain. Brain tissues cannot feel pain. Headache pain arises when blood vessels, nerves and muscles are pressured or stretched. Pain may be felt in the head, eyes and sinuses. Women report twice as many headaches as men. The following suggestions may help avoid headaches:

- Eat regular meals. Many people experience headaches when dieting or skipping a meal.
- Don't drink too much coffee or tea. Headache sufferers often experience a caffeine withdrawal headache when they skip their daily coffee. Limit your caffeine intake to two cups a day.
- Maintain a regular sleeping schedule. Migraine headaches sometimes occur on weekends or holidays because a person sleeps past his normal waking time.
- Refrain from alcoholic beverages or decrease your intake.
- Don't smoke. Smoking increases blood pressure and the pressure on your brain cells.
- Avoid aged cheese and chocolate. Both can cause migraine headaches.
- Keep your hands warm. Applying heat to your hands increases the flow of blood to your brain.
- Foods that contain nitrates (hot dogs, bacon and other cured meats) can cause headaches.
- Avoid Chinese food if it's heavily laced with MSG (Monosodium glutamate). MSG can also cause light-headedness.

Getting Rid Of Simple Headache Pain.
- Try getting some fresh air.
- Lie down for a while.
- Muscle or tension headaches are often relieved by massaging neck muscles. Use of a heating pad or a hot bath also helps.
- Eat a meal. Hunger is sometimes overlooked as a headache cause.
- Take two aspirin. Drink a cup of coffee.

Migraine Headaches. This is the most common type of headache. It occurs when blood vessels in the head enlarge and press against nerves causing pain.

How To Get Relief. Soaking your hands in hot water can relieve a migraine headache, say headache experts.

- When you feel a migraine headache coming on, fill your sink with water as hot as you can stand it.
- Place both hands in the hot water up to your wrists for 30 minutes.

- The heat of the water expands blood vessels in your hands causing more blood to flow there. This draws blood away from bloated arteries in the head which caused the migraine headache pains.
- The hot water also stimulates nerve endings in your hands which sends relaxation signals to your brain.
- The hot water takes concentration away from your pain and directs it elsewhere.

Massaging Away A Migraine.   Many people use a simple remedy to relieve migraine headache pains, says Dr L L Schneider. To relieve a migraine headache take the thumb of one hand and press the palm of the other. Press as firmly as you can, massaging gently. The palm has nerve endings. Pressure on the nerve endings can relieve persistent headache.

Magnesium.   A research study conducted by Dr Kenneth Weaver, Associate Professor of Obstetrics/Gynaecology at East Tennessee State University, showed that supplementing the diet with magnesium may relieve migraine headaches. In a study involving 50 women, Dr Weaver gave them 100 mg of magnesium daily. 80% of the women stopped having migraine headaches or they were reduced in severity. Dr Weaver believes that most people do not get enough magnesium in their diet. You should consult your doctor before taking magnesium.

Migraines And Allergies.   Migraine headaches are often caused by allergies to food, says Dr Ellen Grant of Charing Cross Hospital in London. The doctor researched the cause of migraine headaches in 60 subjects. She found the most common foods contributing to migraine headaches were wheat, oranges, eggs, figs, tea, coffee, chocolate, milk, beef, corn, cane sugar and yeast.

Herbal Remedy.   A controlled clinical study showed that the herb Feverfew, when taken regularly, helped prevent migraines. Feverfew capsules are sold at most health food shops. According to Dr Dean Edell, a prominent San Diego medical doctor, migraine sufferers would have nothing to lose by trying this herb for migraine headache prevention.

Aspirin.   Aspirin may prevent or reduce migraines if taken daily, according to research at Harvard Medical School. The study found that a group of men who took one aspirin daily suffered 20% fewer migraines than those who did not, and those who still reported migraines said that attacks were less severe.

Folk Remedies.   Folk remedies can provide effective, fast relief from headaches and migraines, and they don't produce any side effects. Here are three for you to try:

- Soak your feet in iced water. After a few minutes your feet will begin to feel warm, despite the cold water. Dry them and get into bed. The intense stimulation of your feet from the cold blocks the pain of your headache and you feel better quickly.
- Put some baby oil or handcream on your fingers, then rub the top joint of one thumb hard for a couple of minutes. Do the same with your other thumb, and alternate three to five times. If the pain is severe, 10 minutes of vigorous massage on each thumb may be required. Researchers believe that the pressure on the thumbs creates an overload on the brain, resulting in its pain perception mechanism shutting down.
- A similar way of blocking the pain is to press the roof of your mouth with your thumb, in a different place every few seconds.

HEAD CONGESTION

Try Eucalyptus Leaves.   The vapours of eucalyptus leaves - available in most health food shops - help clear head congestion. Place a few eucalyptus leaves in a pot of boiling water for 5 minutes then turn off the heat. With a towel draped over your head, breathe the vapours. Be careful not to get too close to the steam. It could scald your face.

HEARTBURN

Avoiding Heartburn Discomfort.   Heartburn starts when acid digestive juices and partially digested food back up into the passageway between the mouth and the stomach (called the oesophagus). This irritates sensitive tissues and causes "heartburn" discomfort. Here are practical suggestions for avoiding heartburn:

- Stay away from chocolate, onions and garlic. These items can cause heartburn. Avoid mixing alcoholic beverages and food. It can produce an acid stomach causing heartburn.
- Go easy on your intake of fatty foods. They contribute to heartburn. Stay away from cream sauces, gravies and salad dressings. Use just enough to flavour your food. Stay away from butter. Trim fat from your meat. Eat slowly.
- When eating sit up straight and don't wear tight clothes. Avoid girdles and tight belts.
- After eating don't drink too much coffee. Even decaffeinated coffee can cause heartburn.
- Don't smoke after a meal.
- Don't lie down after a meal. Instead take a short walk.
- Don't eat before bedtime.

Relieving Heartburn Discomfort.
- *Stand.* Merely stand or sit up straight. This forces acid and partially digested food back into the stomach.
- *Milk.* Drinking milk after eating helps combat stomach acid and brings relief.
- *Antacids.* Non-prescriptive antacids available in chemists can be helpful in severe cases.

HEART DISEASE

Kills More Than Cancer. The most common form of heart trouble is atherosclerosis, where the artery linings become clogged with fatty deposits, shutting off the blood flow to the heart. Eating a high-fat diet increases serum cholesterol in the blood and increases the chance of clogged arteries. Other risk factors are high stress, heavy smoking and high blood pressure. Men have three times as many heart attacks as women.

Heart Disease And Cholesterol. It's not just cholesterol level that's important, but the ratio of total cholesterol to HDL, the 'good' cholesterol that helps keep arteries clear, according to Harvard cardiologist, William Castelli. This means that just because your total cholesterol reading is low, your heart isn't necessarily healthy because your HDL level might also be low. Divide your HDL level into your total cholesterol level to find the ratio. A ratio of 4.5 (total cholesterol) to 1 (HDL) or higher means you're at risk of having a heart attack. Below 4.5 is OK and under 3.5 is very good.

Prevention - Sensible Health And Diet Habits.
- Don't smoke.
- Don't become overweight.
- Exercise regularly.
- Eliminate as much stress as possible from your life.
- Cut down on intake of saturated fats.

Reducing Cholesterol In Your Diet. Each 1% drop in blood cholesterol levels yields a 2% reduction in the chance of coronary heart disease, says Dr Richard A Carleton. Thus, a 5% drop in cholesterol brings about a 10% reduction in heart disease risk. A Heart Association panel recommends the following to cut cholesterol levels in your diet:

- Cut fat intake an estimated 20%.
- Reduce saturated (animal) fat to less than 10% of your total calorie intake.
- Limit polyunsaturated (vegetable) fat to 10%.
- Restrict daily cholesterol intake to 250-300 mg.

Staying Alive - Research Studies Worth Considering.
- *Fish Oil.* Studies performed in the Netherlands found that people who eat fish regularly are less likely to die of heart disease than those who do not eat fish. Researchers say that one or two fish dishes per week is a good idea to prevent coronary heart disease. Experts suggest that fish oil reduces fat levels in the blood and makes blood clot more slowly. The types of fish to look out for are mackerel, salmon, sardines, tuna and trout.

   The study showed that the mortality rate for those who consumed at least 14.7 ounces of fish a week was less than half that of those who consumed no fish. The researchers said, by using methods of statistical analysis, that they were able to eliminate other risk factors like cigarette smoking and high blood pressure.

Until this study, the main evidence for low heart disease deaths amongst fish eaters came from studies of Eskimos and Japanese. These groups ate large amounts of fish and had low death rates from heart disease. Researchers say eating fish should be part of a sensible overall diet with lower saturated fats and cholesterol. The studies were published in the New England Journal of Medicine.

- *Aspirin.* Based on a study of 11,965 men who had suffered a heart attack, the Food and Drug Administration has concluded that taking one aspirin a day is a safe and effective way of preventing another heart attack. For those who have suffered a heart attack, taking one aspirin a day can reduce the risk of death by one-fifth. One regular 325 mg aspirin is the normal dosage. Of course, people should continue to see their doctor at regular intervals to assess their progress. Aspirin appears to lessen the chance of a blood clot that can cause a heart attack. The Food and Drug Administration stresses that aspirin therapy for prevention of heart attacks is not a substitute for other preventative measures, such as stopping smoking, eating a sensible diet, losing weight and exercising regularly.
- *Niacin.* Based on a nine year study of 8,300 male heart attack victims, niacin was found to be effective in fighting cholesterol, according to the US National Institutes of Health. The death rate of the heart attack victims taking niacin was about 11% lower than those not taking niacin daily. Niacin may be able to cut the rate of heart disease by 20-30% according to Dr Simeon Margolis, Professor of Medicine and Biological Chemistry at Johns-Hopkins School of Medicine. Niacin is available in most chemists and health food shops.
- *Vitamin C.* A British study found that male heart patients who took one gram of vitamin C daily showed a reduction in cholesterol. Cholesterol contributes to clogging of the arteries. Supplementing the diet with vitamin C can decrease the risk of atherosclerosis, says Dr Brian Libesey, who conducted the study.

Dr Libesey gave 25 patients 1 g of vitamin C daily for six weeks. At the end of the six week period, all heart patients showed a decrease in cholesterol. Total cholesterol fell 12.5%. Foods rich in Vitamin C include citrus fruits and fruit juices, berries, cabbage, green vegetables and potatoes.

- *Lecithin.* A natural substance found in soya beans has been reported to lower cholesterol and other fats in the blood. Dr Lester Morrison from Los Angeles, California gave two tablespoons of lecithin, three times a day (a total of 36 g per day) to 15 people. After three months, 12 of the 15 people showed a significant reduction in blood cholesterol. Other studies have supported Dr Morrison's findings.
- *Alcohol.* Drinking alcoholic beverages in moderation may protect against heart disease, according to Stamford University researchers. A study of 24 men indicated that two drinks a day lessens the risk of atherosclerosis. Yeast and wine contain chromium which raises the level of HDL (good cholesterol) in the blood. Heavy drinking, however, can increase the chance of a heart attack making you more prone to irregular and rapid heartbeat, according to the American Medical Association.
- *Beans.* Preliminary studies show that beans may reduce cholesterol. A 15 month study of 242 people at Sichuan Medical College found that cholesterol levels were lowered after adding beans to the diet for one to three months. Researchers say any kind of beans can be used, including lima beans and kidney beans. They believe that beans inhibit absorption of cholesterol into the body.
- *Garlic.* Research shows garlic may help keep the heart healthy because of its anti-clotting qualities. A study published in the medical journal Lancet examined the diet habits of seven countries. Countries that consumed large amounts of garlic like Greece and Italy had fewer heart disease problems than other countries consuming less garlic. People who cannot stand the smell of garlic can take garlic capsules, available at health food shops. The capsules are odourless and will not affect smell of breath.
- *Stress.* You can reduce the risk of a heart attack by learning how to cope with stress, researchers have found. People who are hostile, aggressive and impatient - commonly referred to as type A behaviour - have the greatest risk of attack, say researchers.
- *Pectin.* Researchers at the University of Florida have found that pectin, when added to the diet in capsule form, can bring down cholesterol levels by between 7% and 20%. Foods rich in pectin are grapefruit and apples.
- *Carrots.* Eating two medium-sized carrots a day can cut your cholesterol by between 10% and 20% say researchers at the US Department of

Agriculture. The cholesterol-fighting ingredient in carrots is calcium pectate, and this is reduced only slightly by cooking.

- *Potassium.* A good supply of potassium in your diet can keep your cholesterol levels down. A study reported in the British Medical Journal showed that patients taking potassium supplements cut their cholesterol by 20% in only two months. You can increase your potassium intake naturally by eating more bananas, raisins, dates, prunes, potatoes and tomatoes.
- *Decaffeinated Coffee.* If you drink several cups of decaffeinated coffee each day, you could increase the 'bad cholesterol' (LDL - low density lipoproteins) in your blood. This is the discovery of a study at Stanford University Lipid Research Clinic in which LDLs were raised by an average of 7% in 181 middle-aged people who drank three to six cups of coffee a day.
- *Exercise And Dieting.* If you are dieting, it's most likely better for your heart if you exercise as well. The reason is that going on a low-fat diet without exercise may reduce your high-density lipoprotein cholesterol (HDL) which is good for your heart. If you exercise as well as diet, you can increase your HDL levels, according to research carried out by Dr Peter Wood at Stanford University and published in the New England Journal of Medicine.

HIATUS HERNIA (DIAPHRAGMATIC HERNIA)

7 Tips For Getting Relief. This condition occurs when a portion of the stomach protrudes above the diaphragm - the muscular wall separating the chest and abdominal cavity. This results in a loss of function of the valve at the bottom of the oesophagus producing heartburn - usually in the area underneath the breast bone. The pain most often occurs at night when in a reclined position. This condition may interrupt sleep. Follow this advice for relief:

- Avoid foods such as coffee, citrus fruit, highly spiced or seasoned foods and chocolate.
- Avoid eating or drinking for several hours before going to bed.
- Avoid tight fitting clothing around the waist.

- Bending should be done with the knees, not the waist, to avoid abdominal pressure.
- Avoid obesity, especially a pot belly.
- Elevate the head of the bed 6 to 8 inches by placing blocks under the front legs of the bed.
- Over-the-counter antacids may neutralise stomach acid and relieve heartburn.

Recent research suggests that lack of fibre in the diet may contribute to flareups. What's more, hiatus hernias are unknown in Africa. Africans eat a strict, high fibre diet.

Studies also show those suffering a hiatus hernia are more prone to gallstones. The reason is not known.

HICCUPS

Home Remedies To Try. Hiccups are a spasm of the diaphragm. The noise is due to air being sucked in and suddenly stopped by tightened vocal chords. Millions of people suffer from hiccups every day.

Several things cause hiccups. These include indigestion, nervousness, exercising too soon after a meal and faulty swallowing of food. Most attacks of hiccups last for less than one hour. Try these remedies for relief:

- Take a deep breath, hold it and blow out slowly.
- Drink a glass of water.
- Apply mild pressure to the eyeballs.
- Swallow a small piece of crushed ice.
- Place an ice bag on the diaphragm just below the rib cage for several minutes.
- Drink a tablespoon of lemon juice.
- Breathe and rebreathe into a paper bag.
- Swallow a teaspoon of honey or vinegar.

Massaging Roof Of Mouth Technique. Massaging the roof of your mouth is the best way to stop hiccups. Here's how it works: Carefully place a swab in your mouth and gently massage the back area of the roof of your mouth where it is soft and fleshy for approximately one minute. This technique is effective in a high percentage of cases.

Charcoal Tablets. A study published in the British Medical Journal showed that activated charcoal tablets relieved hiccups.

Participants in the study chewed charcoal tablets hourly until relief was obtained. Charcoal tablets and capsules are available at most health food shops.

Press On Ear. This method is 90% effective according to Dr Murray Grossan, former chairman of the ear, nose and throat department at Centinela Hospital, USA.

To start, press your chin into your chest while holding a mouthful of water. Then gently press your left ear cavity with your thumb. This calms the vagus nerve and stops the hiccupping.

HOLIDAYS

What Health Care Products Should You Take Along?
- If you wear glasses or contact lenses, take an extra pair, together with a copy of your prescription.
- Prescriptions for all medicines that you use. For medicines you take with you be sure labels clearly indicate what the medicines are.
- A nasal decongestant if you are flying.
- Aspirin or paracetamol. These are the best medication for headache or other pain.
- A diarrhoea treatment.
- A laxative in case of constipation. Don't let more than two days go by without a bowel movement.
- Antiseptics such as TCP and Savlon.
- Tablets for relieving an acid stomach.
- Travel sickness tablets such as Dramamine. Another treatment is ginger root, which is sometimes better because it does not cause drowsiness.
- For sitting out in the sun be sure to take a sun screen.

HUMIDIFIER

May Harbour Bacteria. Humidifier units should be washed at least once a week. Scrub thoroughly with hydrogen peroxide. This will kill the bacteria and fungi that can cause respiratory problems.

HYPERVENTILATION

Tips To Deal With. Hyperventilation is abnormally rapid breathing which decreases carbon dioxide levels in the blood upsetting normal blood chemistry. This can lead to a number of symptoms which often mimic a heart attack. These symptoms include tingling feeling in the fingers, toes and lips, light-headedness, weakness or faintness. Occasionally fainting will occur. Hyperventilation attacks may last half an hour or longer and may recur several times in a 24-hour period.

Most often hyperventilation is a response to stress, anxiety and emotional upset. Fatigue and excessive alcohol consumption can contribute to the problem. The following tips will relieve hyperventilation:

- *Breathe In A Paper Bag*
  1. Cover your mouth and nose completely with a paper bag.
  2. Breathe slowly into the bag and rebreathe the air. The air in the bag contains additional carbon dioxide.
  3. Breathe slowly in and out of the bag at least 10 times.
  4. Put the bag aside and breathe normally a few minutes.
  5. Repeat the process until the symptoms diminish or disappear.
  6. If symptoms return, repeat the process as often as needed.
- *Relax And Stay Calm.* Slow your breathing down. The more tense you are the faster you breathe. Try to take one breath about every six seconds.
- *Stay Away From Caffeine.* Caffeine stimulates your entire body and mind. This can aggravate tension and cause breathing to become faster.

HYPOTHERMIA (CHILLING OF THE ENTIRE BODY)

Ways To Help The Victim.
1. Bring the victim into a warm room as soon as possible.
2. Remove wet clothing.
3. Wrap victim in warm blanket, towels or additional clothing.
4. Seek medical attention promptly.

IMPOTENCE

May Be Caused By Vitamin Deficiency. Impotence is most often caused by psychological factors. In only 10% of cases is the cause physical. Impotency may also be a side effect of prescription medications. Deficiencies in zinc and vitamins A and C may bring about impotence too. Despite popular belief, vitamin E has no effect on this condition.

Sarsaparilla tea has been used by Indians in Mexico as a sexual stimulant for centuries. This tea is available in most health food shops.

A herb called yohimbine, from the bark of the yohimb tree, is used in many countries to restore function and desire in men. Yohimbine is said to dilate blood vessels and help to create and maintain an erection. In a study reported in The Lancet, a group of sufferers took either yohimbine or a placebo pill. 62% of yohimine takers had an improvement in sexual function, while only 16% of those taking the placebo did.

Low-Fat Diet. Dr Padma-Nathan of the University of Southern California suggests that over 50% of impotency may be caused by clogged arteries leading to the penis. Therefore the same kind of diet that contributes to a healthy heart may help men to avoid the problem of impotency.

INCONTINENCE

Stress Incontinence. This is particularly common in elderly women and means that some urine is lost, for example, when sneezing, coughing or lifting. One remedy is to do the following Kegel exercise: tense the pelvic floor (as if you are holding back a stool) for 10 seconds, then relax for 10 seconds. Do this for 10 minutes, three times a day. You should persevere for about three months before any improvement is felt. Sometimes a drug will be prescribed to tighten the neck of the bladder and this should be taken in conjunction with doing the exercises.

INDIGESTION (SIMPLE)

9 Suggestions For Avoiding Indigestion. Simple indigestion is normally brought about by overeating, eating too fast, not chewing food properly, eating spicy or fatty foods or foods that cause an allergic reaction. Indigestion is often due to psychological factors like worry, frustration and emotional upset. Simple indigestion causes an uncomfortable feeling of fullness and slight pain in the stomach. If symptoms linger a doctor should be consulted for diagnosis. The following suggestions should help avoid problems.

- Eat meals at a leisurely pace. Don't gobble food or eat at stand-up counters.
- Don't water-log food. Drink liquids before or after meals - not during.
- Eat meals in a comfortable, relaxing atmosphere. Don't discuss problems or conflicts while eating. Wait at least one hour.
- Avoid smoking before, during and after meals.
- Don't wear tight clothes around your mid-section.
- Eat meals at regular intervals. This helps the stomach secrete digestive juices.
- Avoid large, heavy meals, especially those spicy and heavy in fat.
- Drink a glass of milk between meals. This will help avoid excess stomach acid.
- Avoid chocolate or gum. They may stimulate stomach acid.

Relieving Discomfort.
Indigestion can be soothed by effervescents like Alka-Seltzer, which work quickly to neutralise stomach acids: your best bet for occasional indigestion, says Dr Arnold Levy of the American Digestive Disease Society.

That bloated feeling of gas and heartburn is best treated by anti-gas antacids available from your chemist. These products help break up gas bubbles. (If you require antacids constantly for symptom relief you should visit a doctor immediately.)

There are also several natural remedies:

- *Fennel.* Fennel is an old-fashioned remedy for indigestion. It is recommended in the book "Back to Eden" as a remedy for gas and acid stomach. This herb can be sprinkled on food to prevent stomach gas.
- *Aniseed.* The book "Nature's Healing Agents" recommends aniseed for a sour stomach. The aniseed can be chewed or ground and sprinkled on food.
- *Mint.* Both peppermint and spearmint have been used for years as a remedy for indigestion. A cup of peppermint tea is a good remedy. It will soothe the stomach.

These natural ingredients are available at health food shops.

Breathing Exercise. To combat symptoms of stomach acid, try this abdominal breathing exercise, says Dr Nels Olson, from the University of Michigan: push out your stomach with each breath rather than expanding your chest.

Activated Charcoal For Stomach Gas. Activated charcoal capsules, available at most health food shops, can relieve stomach gas. (Also good for diarrhoea and hiccups.) Charcoal absorbs gas like a sponge. It can also absorb intestinal bacteria that can cause gas. Many people prefer charcoal capsules to any other product for stomach discomfort. If you haven't tried charcoal capsules you are missing out on one of the best stomach aids available.

Indigestion And Soapy Film. Soapy film on dishes and silverware can cause problems in your digestive system. Detergent film can build up in your system and cause problems over a period of years.

Avoid Detergent Irritants.
- Use a minimum of soap when washing dishes.
- Rinse everything thoroughly after washing. Be especially careful with items such as forks where residue can lodge in small areas.
- Re-rinse any silverware that has a soapy taste.

INGROWING TOE-NAILS

4 Tips For Home Care. This is the growth of a toe-nail into the soft tissue of a toe. It is most often caused by improper fitting shoes. Another cause is improper cutting of the toe-nails. Most people cut toe-nails to fit the contour of the toe. This can cause trouble. The toe-nail should be cut straight across without any curves. Do the following for relief:

- Soak the toe in warm salt water. Remove the dead, granulated tissue with scissors.
- Wear a cut-out-toe shoe.
- Paint the ingrown part of the nail with a 1% solution of gentian violet.
- Slip a piece of cotton soaked in castor oil under the edge of the ingrown toe-nail to keep it pointing upwards and out.

INSECT BITES

3 Tips For Avoiding Insect Bites. Many people experience severe allergic reactions to insect bites. These reactions could include dizziness, nausea, diarrhoea, itching and difficulty breathing. If you have a serious reaction to an insect bite see a doctor immediately. Follow these rules to avoid problems:

- When you're outdoors cooking or eating be careful. Food and drink often attract insects.
- Don't wear open shoes or loose fitting clothes. Avoid bright coloured clothing that may attract insects.
- Be careful when gardening. Wear a hat and long sleeved shirt, boots and gloves.

What To Do When Bitten.
- Scrape out any stingers with your fingernail or a blunt knife. Do not try to pull the sting out. Squeezing will only inject more venom into the wound.
- Wash the bite with soap and water. Then apply antiseptic.
- Apply an ice pack and/or a paste of baking soda and water to relieve the pain.
- Elevate the arm or leg to reduce fluid retention and swelling.

Using Your Antiperspirant. The active ingredient in antiperspirants sold in chemists is aluminium chloride. This ingredient relieves itching, pain and inflammation from insect bites, says Dr Walter Shelley of the Medical College of Ohio. The aluminium chloride dries the skin and kills the bacteria to prevent infection. The antiperspirant should be applied to insect bites about once every 10 hours.

Simple Home Remedy. Rubbing meat tenderiser dampened with water on insect bites and stings reduces inflammation and stops pain.

IRON

Women Need More. The monthly blood loss during menstruation may cause an iron deficiency in women, according to an article in the US Federal Government's FDA Consumer. A loss of 10 to 15 mg of iron occurs during a typical menstrual period. About 10% of women may need twice that much, including many wearing IUDs.

Fatigue - A Common Symptom. Iron deficiency can cause fatigue, headache and pale complexion. Increasing evidence indicates that even a mild depletion of iron reserves may impair mental and physical performance.

Daily Iron Needs. The National Research Council recommends that women consume 18 mg of iron daily. The body only absorbs about 10% of the iron in food.
- Vitamin C helps absorption. Dr James Cook, Professor of Medicine at the University of Kansas Medical Centre, found that taking 66 mg of vitamin C with meals can increase absorption of iron up to 500%.
- Drinking tea interferes with iron absorption because it contains tannic acid and phylates. Antacids also diminish iron absorption.

ITCHING

3 Suggestions For Relieving Itching Skin.

- According to an article in the Journal of the American Medical Association, 60 mg of iron, taken three times a day relieved itching in persons suffering severe itching.
- A 20 minute, lukewarm bath with bath oil added is very good for dry, itching skin, says Dr B Allen Flaxman. The warm water tends to open pores allowing the oil into the skin bringing comfort and relief from itching.
- Try soaking in a warm bath containing half a cupful of baking soda.

JET LAG

Anti-Jet Lag Diet. The Anti-Jet Lag diet is helping countless numbers of travellers quickly adjust their body's internal clocks to new time zones. It is also being used by persons working alternate day and night shifts and who have to rotate their working hours periodically.

How To Avoid Jet Lag.

1. Determine breakfast time at your destination on the day of arrival.
2. Start your Anti-Jet Lag diet three days before your departure date. On day one 'feast'. Eat heartily with a high-protein breakfast and lunch and a high carbohydrate dinner. Drink no coffee except between 3 and 5pm. On day two, fast on light meals of salads, light soups, fruit and juices. Again, no coffee except between 3 and 5pm. On day three, 'feast' again. On day four, departure day, fast. If you drink caffeinated beverages have them in the morning when travelling west or between 6 and 11pm when travelling east.
3. Break your final fast at breakfast time at your destination. Have no alcohol on the plane. If your flight is long enough sleep until normal breakfast time at your destination, but no later. Stay awake and active.
4. Continue your meals according to meal times at your destination.

JOB BOREDOM

Overcoming Boredom.
- Change the way you go to work. If you drive your car, take a different route - a more scenic one. If you go to work using public transport consider joining a car pool.
- When at work do the most difficult tasks first.
- Move your desk or sit at a different location.
- Seek new assignments and new responsibility.
- Volunteer for activities outside of work such as badminton or football teams.
- Change your work habits. Go somewhere different for lunch or try eating lunch with new employees.

JOCK ITCH

3 Suggestions For Relief. Jock itch is a fungal infection around the genital area. It strikes males who regularly engage in vigorous exercise. Moisture and friction cause the fungus to grow.
- Quickly change sweaty and soiled clothing.
- Wear jockey type shorts rather than the baggier boxer shorts.
- Sprinkle the affected area with Tinactin powder after bathing.

JOINT INJURIES

Home Remedies For Minor Problems.
- *Rest.* Stop using the injured joint as soon as you feel pain, says Dr Charles Bull.
- *Ice.* Place a towel over the injured joint and apply an ice pack over the towel.
- *Compression.* Wrap an elastic bandage over the ice and around the injured part to limit swelling. Leave the ice pack and bandage in place for 20 minutes of wrapping and 20 minutes of unwrapping for a total of three hours.
- *Elevation.* Position the injured part so it is above the level of your heart so that gravity will help drain excess fluids.

- Continue treatment for up to 24 hours.
- Consult a doctor if your pain is severe or lasts more than one week.

KIDNEY STONES

You Can Prevent Kidney-stones. Kidney-stones are most prevalent among white men between the ages of 20 and 30. The 'stones' are calcium oxalate crystals which form inside the kidney. Symptoms are severe pain between the stomach and the groin, frequent, painful urination and the passing of blood with the urine. If you are susceptible to kidney-stones, they may recur every three or four years. You can prevent this happening by altering your diet.
- Drink at least 10 glasses of water a day.
- Reduce salt intake.
- Do not take excessive amounts of food high in oxalate, such as spinach, rhubarb, black pepper or nuts.
- Do not eat excessive amounts of meat.
- Limit vitamin C intake to 500 - 1,000 mg per day.
- Limit calcium intake to 1,000 mg per day.

KNOCKED OUT TOOTH

What To Do. Wrap the knocked out tooth in a cool wet cloth. Take the victim and the tooth to the dentist as soon as possible. A dentist can often reimplant the tooth with a high degree of success.

LAUGHTER

May Fight Disease And Pain. Laughter stimulates the brain to produce hormones that fight disease and pain, according to Dr William Fry of Stanford Medical School in California. Laughter is like an inoculation against disease. Without laughter, people get sick more often. Hormones generated by laughter reduce tension - a major cause of pain. Laughter is also good for guilt and depression.

LEG CRAMPS

Tips That May Help. Leg cramps due to muscle spasms are a common problem, especially amongst older people. Cramps most often happen at night. The discomfort can be relieved by walking or moving the leg. Also consider these nutrients. It is best to check with your doctor before taking these supplements:

- *Calcium.* Supplementing your diet with about 900 mg of calcium per day can ease leg cramps caused by muscle spasms.
- *Vitamin E.* Supplementing the diet with 100 IUs of vitamin E with each meal may help ease leg cramps.
- *Magnesium.* You may be lacking magnesium in your diet. You can increase intake by eating more beans, nuts, bananas, potatoes, whole wheat and soy products.
- *Potassium.* Increasing your intake of potassium may help: this mineral is found in fish, tomatoes, raisins, milk and orange juice, as well as bananas and potatoes.

LICE

How To Prevent And Treat. Lice are parasites that infest the body, especially hairy parts. They often cause severe itching and tiny red marks on the skin. Lice are often carriers of typhus.

How Transmitted. Lice can be transmitted by personal contact, use of a borrowed comb, brush, hat or other clothing. The white lice eggs attach to the hair and mature in 3 to 14 days.

Treatment. A safe insecticide in cream form or lotion available at a chemist should be applied to all hairy surfaces and rubbed into the scalp at night. In the morning shampoo thoroughly. Repeat this treatment a week later to catch any lice that have survived or have been newly born.

Tips To Prevent. Periodically sterilise hats, brushes, combs and other clothing that goes on the head. Thoroughly launder bed linen and towels. Avoid all body contact until lice disappear.

LIVER SPOTS

Tips To Avoid Liver Spots. These are dark patches of skin caused by the skin's exposure to the sun's radiation, and have nothing to do with the liver. They are especially prevalent in women over the age of 40. Here are some ways you can prevent them.

- Don't sunbathe.
- If you have to go out in the sun, wear a sun screen with a protection factor higher than 15.
- Wear a hat, long sleeves and trousers when you know you are going to be exposed to the sun for a long time.

Removal of Liver Spots. The best method of removal is for a dermatologist to freeze the patch with liquid nitrogen - this destroys the pigments in the top layer of skin, leaving a white patch which will return to your natural skin colour after a few months.

LIVING LONGER

What Can You Do Now? The American Longevity Association has ten tips to help you live to be 100 or over. Here are the Association's recommendations:

- Substitute fish for meat as often as possible. Fish contains oils that may prevent heart attacks.
- Use fish oils and olive oils in salads and cooking. Research has shown that these oils lower cholesterol.
- Substitute vegetables for meat and dairy products.
- Increase your intake of food high in beta-carotene such as carrots, spinach, broccoli and cantaloup. This helps prevent cancer.
- Stay on a basic low-fat diet to prevent heart disease and cancer.
- Keep your calorific intake and weight low to help slow ageing.

- To help keep body tissues healthy eat more foods high in vitamin C (citrus fruits, green vegetables, green peppers, etc).
- Eat food high in vitamin E (vegetable oils and grains), zinc (pork, pumpkin seeds) and selenium (bran, tuna fish).
- Substitute hard water for soft water. Also, use a charcoal filter to help eliminate chlorine from your water and remove cancer-causing materials.
- Don't smoke.

10 Old-Fashioned Rules. According to Dr L L Schneider in his book "Old-Fashioned Health Remedies", the ten rules for longer life are as follows:

1. Get 7 to 8 hours sleep every night.
2. Eat three well-balanced meals per day.
3. Eat bulk foods and mineral and vitamin enriched foods daily.
4. Cut down on sugary foods and chemically-treated foods.
5. Get sunshine and fresh air each day if possible.
6. Drink a few glasses of fresh water each day.
7. Do not smoke. Stay away from people who do smoke.
8. Avoid alcoholic drinks except rarely and even then only in moderation.
9. Exercise naturally every day. Walking, swimming or gardening are good.
10. Use laughter to banish anxiety and fear. Let every day be joyous.

LONELINESS

4 Things That Can Help.
- Go to shopping centres frequently. They are good places to meet people. In eating areas, it's especially easy to strike up conversations, says psychiatrist Robert Amstadter.
- Send for free catalogues and literature. In a short time your letterbox will be brimming with reading material; and with mail streaming in regularly, you'll be kept too busy reading to dwell on your loneliness.
- Check out car boot sales and weekend flea markets. Not only will you meet a variety of people - you might even find some bargains.
- Call radio chat shows. As a regular listener and caller, you'll soon feel like you're a part of the show family.

MARITAL CHEATING

About 1 In Every 4 Spouses Cheat. Marital cheating can be bad for your health when your mate finds out about it. Researchers say that about 26% of husbands and 21% of wives have love affairs with other partners.

MEDICINES

How To Tell If Spoiled. Always check expiry date. Then check for signs of deterioration as follows:

- *Solutions And Liquids.* Odour, taste and colour should be the same as when originally purchased.
- *Pills And Tablets.* They should retain their original size, weight and colour. Splits, cracks and chips are a sign of decay. Also watch out for any unusual odour.
- *Capsules.* Capsules should not be too soft. They should not stick together. They should not crack under pressure.
- *Ointments.* Should be the same as when purchased. Ointments should not be harder or softer than when they were originally purchased.

MEMORY

Lecithin And Memory Improvement. A study conducted at the National Institute of Mental Health showed that lecithin significantly improved memory and recall in normal healthy people. After taking lecithin, volunteers were able to remember a sequence of unrelated words more quickly. This study was published in the Life Sciences Medical Journal. Lecithin is available in health food shops.

Diet. Studies by experts at Boston University School of Medicine and Columbia University School of Medicine have shown that your memory and intelligence can be improved by eating more healthily. Specifically, you should ensure that the food you eat supplies you with a regular intake of folic acid, iron, calcium, magnesium, zinc, copper, lecithin, tyrosine, choline, tryptophan and vitamins C, B1, B2, B3, B5, B6 and B12. All these nutrients help the body make the chemicals that help the brain work. Your diet should, therefore, include milk, bread and cereal products, lean meat, poultry and seafood, together with plenty of fresh fruit and vegetables. Eggs may also be included - they are high in lecithin, choline, zinc and B vitamins.

Dr Stephen Schoenthaler, a specialist in nutrition and brain function at California State University carried out some experiments on the brain power of students. A more nutritious diet increased one group's test results by an average of 16%, while another group were given multi-vitamin tablets for several months; the result of this was that those previously deficient in minerals increased their IQs by up to 25 points.

Mid-Afternoon Snacks. Another study, by Tufts University School of Nutrition, shows that you can boost your memory and concentration by having a mid-afternoon snack, such as a chocolate bar or yoghurt.

MENTAL HEALTH

Problems Can Strike Anyone. No segment of our society is immune from mental illness. It can affect anyone - rich or poor, educated or not educated. It can strike at almost any age.

The picture is not bleak, however. People do recover from mental illness. There are some famous examples including President Abraham Lincoln, novelist Virginia Wolfe, US Senator Thomas Eagleton, popular singer Rosemary Clooney and professional golfer Bert Yancey. All suffered from mental illness but totally recovered.

Abraham Lincoln, for example, suffered from severe depression. Only after he overcame this affliction did he attain the Presidency and become one of the world's most outstanding leaders. Lincoln is not alone in having achieved great success despite struggles with mental illness. There are thousands of cases of men and women who have suffered from mental illness - have recovered and risen to great heights of success and happiness.

If you or someone else is affected by any type of mental illness do not get discouraged. The vast majority of people recover and go on to lead happy, productive lives. Moreover, most people during their lifetime experience difficult periods that can be considered some form of mental illness.

Warning Signals Of Mental Illness. Whilst not definite signs of mental disturbances, the following signs of trouble can sometimes help you identify someone who needs help.

- Is the person acting differently from usual? Can you link this change in behaviour to something that has happened recently?
- Does the person seem to be excessively withdrawn and depressed? Are hobbies, friends and relatives ignored suddenly? Is there a feeling this person has begun to lose confidence? Depressive illnesses have many symptoms similar to these.
- Does the individual complain of episodes of extreme, almost uncontrollable anxiety? Is this anxiety unrelated to any normal concern such as a child's illness or a backlog of bills? Anxiety having no recognisable cause is a sign of emotional difficulty.
- Does the person become aggressive, rude or abusive over minor incidents? Are there remarks about individuals or groups out to get him? This is an indication that some help may be required.
- Is there any change in the person's habits such as eating, sleeping or grooming? Suddenly, has the individual almost stopped eating? Conversely, has the person started eating or drinking a lot in a compulsive manner? Either sleeplessness or a lot of sleep can be indicators if they are excessive.

Any of these signals, if they continue for any length of time may call for professional help.

What To Do In Emergency Situations. If a person becomes violent, gets completely out of control or even tries to commit suicide, there are several things you can do.

- Call a doctor. Call the person's family doctor if he has one. If not, get the person to a hospital where there are doctors on duty in an emergency unit. You may have to call an ambulance to get the person there. Call the emergency services on 999. Also, many clergy are trained to deal with emergencies or they can refer you to the right help.
- If the victim is already in treatment, call his therapist.

116

- Call the Samaritans or Alcoholics Anonymous in your area. The numbers will be in the Yellow Pages or you can ask the operator for help. These telephone lines are often manned around the clock.
- In crisis emergencies call the police. Often the police are the best equipped, most available resource, especially when a crime has been committed or when there is a strong possibility that the person may do physical injury to himself or others.

Treatment Methods.   Here are some of the modern methods of treatment to help overcome problems.

Short-Term Psychotherapy. This approach is used when a problem seems to be brought on by some event or episode in life such as a death in the family, divorce or physical illness. Even good news can sometimes cause a severe upset. A job promotion or move to a better home are good examples. The goal of the therapy is to help iron out the problem as quickly as possible. Often this takes only a few visits.

Family Therapy. In this method, the whole family is interviewed to help determine the root cause of the problem. Perhaps a son needs to be with his father more. A mother may be spending too much time worrying about things that would be less of a problem if she could see them in a different light. If the family therapist can lead the family members to see each other in a new light, their behaviour towards one another can improve and their problems begin to fade.

Group Therapy. Group therapy takes place when a small group of people gather to discuss their common problems under the guidance of a therapist. The group members help each other with their individual problems. The therapist guides the conversation into useful directions, offers advice if needed and points out things the group members might otherwise miss.

Other Treatments. There are other kinds of psychotherapy. Some involve an in-depth study of the underlying causes of a problem that started in childhood. Other therapies deal more with the person's life here and now. Everyday situations are looked at to help the patient better understand himself.

Where To Go For Help: Paying For The Services. If you are financially able to pay for psychological counselling, there are a large number of qualified professionals listed in your telephone book. You have a choice of going to a psychiatrist, who is a trained medical doctor, or a psychologist.

The Most Common Types Of Mental Problems. The most common problems in today's society are anxiety and depression. Each of these problems is described below.

Anxiety. Anxiety is a fearful anticipation of something. The fear may be real or imagined. Either way it feels the same. Everyone at one time or another has experienced mild anxiety. It is only when these feelings of anxiety become severe that they cause problems. To feel anxiety is to feel fearful, scared, jittery, edgy, concerned, worried, helpless, insecure, uptight. Most of these feelings involve uncertainty over one's personal safety. The intensity of the anxiety depends on the real or imagined severity of the impending loss, the closeness of the threat and the importance of the loss to the individual.

When we experience anxiety, certain hormones, especially adrenalin, shoot through our bodies and can cause physical symptoms such as sweaty palms, rapid pulse, increase in blood pressure, dizziness and a wide variety of other physical sensations. Severe anxiety is often described as panic, where a person can feel disoriented, detached, frantic, with weird feelings and sensations. They may think they are going crazy or will lose their mind or will lose control of themselves. This can be a very disabling problem. The feeling of panic can be so severe it can cause a condition referred to as agoraphobia, where the person is afraid of leaving the home for fear of having a panic attack. Anxiety and panic conditions can often be successfully treated through psychotherapy. Complete professional treatment programmes for those suffering anxiety, panic and phobias are available throughout the country.

People suffering severe anxiety are often prescribed anti-anxiety medications such as valium, librium or xanax. These medications are highly effective in controlling anxiety during the time the person is solving the root cause of the problem through some kind of therapy.

Avoid Sugar. Three studies by the US National Institute of Mental Health revealed that 75% of patients suffering from anxiety and panic disorders had a dramatic increase in anxiety after eating sugar. Moreover, 50% of people not suffering from anxiety also experience a higher level of anxiety after eating sugar. The sugar consumed during the study was equivalent to 1 to 2 slices of cake or 1 to 2 chocolate bars daily. Researchers suspect that sugar may cause the body to release too much of the hormone adrenaline. Adrenaline is the major culprit in causing physical reactions and panic attacks.

Caffeine. According to an article in the New England Journal of Medicine, caffeine triggers the release of adrenalin which can cause heart arrhythmia, stress and panic reactions.

Depression. As many as 1 in 5 of us will experience depression some time in our lives. Women suffer depression twice as often as men. Depression, unlike occasional blue days everyone experiences, is a persistant disorder. It can bring on physical as well as mental symptoms.

Some common symptoms of depression include:
- Getting little or no pleasure out of anything in life.
- Losing interest in your job, family life, hobbies or even sex.
- Experiencing frequent and unexplained crying spells.
- Feeling a loss of self-esteem.
- Becoming unusually irritable.
- Having trouble sleeping, especially waking up at early hours and not feeling well.
- Difficulty concentrating and remembering.
- Experiencing physical pain you can't pin down.
- Loss of appetite and constipation.

Depression in most cases can be easily diagnosed and successfully treated. New, effective anti-depressant drugs can shorten the course of depression. These drugs may help people function day to day, keeping their jobs and relationships intact.

The most widely used anti-depressant class of drugs are called tricyclics. Experts say that about 80% of those on the right dosage of tricyclic drugs eventually get better. These medications are usually taken before going to bed and provide relief throughout the day. These anti-depressant drugs usually take about two weeks before they are effective in helping lift depression.

Doctors also suggest certain lifestyle changes that can help avoid and relieve depression. Among these are regular exercising, thinking positive thoughts, maintaining social contacts as much as possible, eating a balanced diet, participating in hobbies and recreational activities and maintaining close family ties.

MICROWAVE OVEN SAFETY

Microwave Ovens And Your Health. Microwave radiation can heat body tissue the same way it heats food. Exposure to high levels of microwaves can cause a painful burn. The lense of the eye is particularly sensitive to intense heat, and exposure to high levels of microwaves can cause cataracts. Likewise the testes are very sensitive to changes in temperature. Accidental exposure to high levels of microwaves can alter or kill sperm production causing temporary sterility. Less is known about what happens to people exposed to low levels of microwaves. Research is continuing in this area.

Checking Microwave Ovens For Leakage. There is little cause for concern about excess microwaves leaking from ovens unless the door hinges, latches or seals are damaged.

If there is some problem and you believe your oven might be leaking, contact the oven manufacturer or a microwave repair service. Most oven manufacturers will arrange for your oven to be checked.

Tips On Microwave Oven Operation.
- Follow the manufacturer's instruction manual recommending operating procedures and safety precautions for your own model.
- Don't operate an oven if the door does not close firmly or is bent, warped or otherwise damaged.
- Never operate an oven if you have reason to believe it will continue to operate when the door is open.
- Don't stand directly against an oven and don't allow children to do this for long periods of time whilst in operation.

MOULD

Source Of Harmful Bacteria. Mould on fruits can be a source of harmful bacteria. It can also cause allergies. The mould goes much deeper than what appears on the fruit. It is a good idea to dispose of fruit containing any kind of mould at all.

MORNING SICKNESS

3 Suggestions To Help Avoid. Morning sickness is the term used to describe the feeling of nausea that occurs in the early weeks of pregnancy. Try the following for relief:

- Eat before getting out of bed in the morning. If you cannot eat a full breakfast, then tea and biscuits are the next best thing.
- Instead of eating three regular meals a day, try eating several small meals.
- After eating lie down for about 20 minutes.

Vitamin B-6. Many women have reported relief by supplementing their diet with vitamin B-6. Dr Dean Edell, a San Diego physician, recommends taking no more than 75-100 mg per day. Check with your doctor first.

Ginger Root Capsules. Ginger root capsules are commonly used for motion sickness. But many women take them for the relief of morning sickness, according to Dr Edell. Ginger root capsules are available at most health food shops. Check with your doctor first.

Morning sickness may be a good sign. Studies show that women having morning sickness are more likely to have a healthy baby.

MOSQUITO BITES

2 Suggestions For Avoiding Bites. Mosquito bites should be avoided. Mosquitoes can also spread encephalitis (inflammation of the brain) and yellow fever. Try these suggestions for avoiding mosquito bites:

- Vitamin B-1. Researchers at Lake Superior State College in Michigan conducted a study on 60 volunteers. Thirty of the volunteers took a vitamin B-1 supplement, and the other 30 were given a fake pill. Volunteers then went outdoors, keeping track of any mosquito bites. Those who took the vitamin B-1 supplement reported fewer insect bites. Your body's supply of vitamin B-1 can be depleted by excess intake of sugar and alcohol. Foods rich in vitamin B-1 include brown rice, brewer's yeast, wheat germ and fish.
- Refined sugar. Eliminating refined sugar from your diet causes mosquitoes not to bite you, according to William Dufty, author of the book "Sugar Blues". Eliminate refined sugar from your diet for at least a year and mosquitos will leave you alone, says Dufty.

When refined sugar is eaten, the skin lets off a sweet scent that attracts mosquitoes. When sugar is eliminated the skin no longer produces this scent. Mosquitoes won't bother you.

MOUTH ULCERS

Helpful Suggestions To Stop Flareups. Mouth ulcers are shallow, open sores in the mouth. The inside of the sore is white surrounded by a red border. Some people get them regularly - every month or even every week. The sores usually go away in 7 to 14 days and leave no scars. The exact cause of mouth ulcers is unknown, but some researchers believe they are brought about by sensitivity to certain foods or emotional stress. The following tips may help to solve mouth ulcer problems:

- *Zinc.* Taking 50 mg of zinc daily has been reported to prevent and shorten the duration of mouth ulcers.
- *Vitamin Deficiency.* Studies by the Institute for Dental Research have shown that some people who get mouth ulcers may be deficient in iron, folic acid and vitamin B-12.
- *Acidophilus.* Many people have reported that taking acidophilus capsules several times a day with meals tends to prevent and clear up mouth ulcers. This friendly bacteria (lactobacillus acidophilus) is also in yoghurt.
- *Tetracycline.* Some doctors prescribe the antibiotic tetracycline for mouth ulcers. The treatment involves dissolving a capsule in an ounce of warm

water and swishing the mixture in the mouth for 10 minutes, repeating several times a day for about five days. The tetracycline mixture is sometimes applied with a cotton bud.

- *Myrrh.* Several chemists recommend a herb called myrrh to treat mouth ulcers. It can be purchased in most health food shops in an alcohol solution. Simply apply with a cotton top. Just touch the centre of the sore. The soreness should subside and healing should follow.
- *Silver Nitrate.* Treating mouth ulcers with silver nitrate shortens the course of the sore, says Dr John E Eichenlaub. Simply moisten the tip of a cotton bud with 10% silver nitrate solution (available at a chemist). Hold it on the mouth ulcer for 5 to 10 seconds then rinse with a little water. After that, wash your mouth thoroughly with a mild salt solution 3 or 4 times a day (half a teaspoon in a glass of warm water).
- *Food Allergy.* Many doctors believe mouth ulcers are caused by an allergic reaction to food. Dr C W M Wilson, from Dublin, Ireland, noticed that most people who suffer mouth ulcers are also allergic to certain foods. The foods most often causing mouth ulcers are coffee, tea, wheat germ, pork, turnips, cabbage, eggs and milk. Dr Wilson believes the burning and tangy sensations preceding the sores signals consumption of an allergic food. Other foods associated with mouth ulcer flareups include citrus fruits and walnuts.
- *Use A Soft Tooth Brush.* An experiment on a group of patients experiencing occasional mouth ulcers showed that when pin pricks were made in their mouths, ulcers formed where the prick was made. Use a soft tooth brush to avoid any scratching or other trauma to the mouth while brushing your teeth. This alone can significantly alleviate mouth ulcer problems.

NAILS

How To Care For Them.
- *Brittle Nails.* Keep fingernails well moisturised. Use nail polish remover as little as possible. Buffing nails smoothes them and removes debris. Avoid contact with detergents and chemicals. Supplementing diet with iron may help. Foods rich in iron include dark green, leafy vegetables, fish, pulses and whole grains.

The B vitamin, biotin can make nails stronger and thicker and less likely to split, according to research at Columbia University School of Medicine and the F Hoffmann-La Roche Inc drug company in Switzerland. Natural sources of biotin include cauliflower, lentils, soybeans, peanut butter and milk.

- *Hangnails.* Cut off with sharp scissors. Proper moisturising and wearing gloves while doing work is the best way to prevent hangnails.
- *Ingrown Toe-nails.* Cut toe-nails straight across so there are no edges to grow into the flesh. In severe cases consult your doctor. (Also see the section on ingrowing toe-nails.)

NASAL CONGESTION

Unclogging The Nose. Nasal congestion occurs when blood vessels in the nose enlarge, taking up space in the nasal cavity. This restricts the amount of air allowed in for easy breathing.

- *Hot Soup.* One study showed that hot soup speeded the flow of mucus out of the nose. Adding cayenne pepper and onion may hasten relief.
- *Eucalyptus.* Place eucalyptus leaves in a pan of boiling water for 5 minutes. Turn the heat off and, with a towel draped around your head, lean over the pan and breathe in the herbal vapours. Be careful not to burn yourself.
- *Nasal Decongestants.* Nasal drops, sprays and inhalers work by shrinking swollen blood vessels in the nose. Over-use tends to 'tire' these blood vessels, making congestion worse over time.

NECK TENSION

Simple Exercise May Help. Muscles in the neck area can become tense due to stress, working in an uncomfortable position and many other reasons. Try this exercise for relief:

1. Roll your head around your shoulders. Roll first one way then the other.
2. Pull your chin in as far as you can. At the same time, stretch the back of your neck.
3. Lean your head on one side and then another. Hold the cords of your neck tightly.

Posture.
- Avoid straining your neck by thrusting your head forward when sitting at a desk, driving or watching the television.
- Hold your head up straight when you walk.
- Prop yourself up with pillows while reading in bed.
- Don't sleep on your stomach - it strains your neck because it is pushed to one side.
- Don't sleep on pillows that are too high.

Vibrator. Massaging the neck with a good quality vibrator is one of the best ways to relieve neck tension. Vibrate the neck muscles on each side of the vertebrae and along the top of the shoulders. The intense vibration exhausts the muscles to the point of complete relaxation. After vibrating, apply alcohol or an analgesic for a more lasting effect. Regular vibrating treatments will control neck tension.

NERVOUS TENSION

2 Simple Tips To Relieve Tension.

Massage Hands. Massaging the web structure of the hand between the finger and thumb helps relieve nervous tension, according to Dr L L Schneider in his book "Old-Fashioned Health Remedies That Work Best". Apply hand cream for lubrication before starting. There are many nerve endings in the webbing between thumb and fingers. Start with the left hand. Repeat on the right hand for 5 minutes, twice a day or until tension is relieved.

Anti-Tension Breathing Exercise.
1. While standing, place both hands high on the rib cage as near the arm pits as possible.
2. Press inward as far as possible with both hands at the same time.
3. Suddenly release both hands at the same time.
4. Inhale deeply holding the breath for 5 seconds. Repeat this exercise 3 to six times.

Relief Of Tension Headaches. Here are some suggestions to relieve headaches caused by tension from Dr Seymour Diamond, executive director of the US National Headache Foundation.

- *Shoulder Rolls.* With your arms loose at your side, slowly rotate both shoulders forward three times, then rotate them backwards.
- *Shoulder Stretch.* Relax your shoulders; clasp your hands together in front and lift your arms slowly towards the ceiling, keeping your elbows straight and pulling outward with your arms. Slowly bring your arms back to the starting position and repeat this exercise twice. Next, clasp your arms behind your back and lift them slowly upwards, keeping your shoulders loose and elbows straight. Gently lower your arms to the starting position and do the exercise twice more.
- *Eye Stretches.* Sit at a table, resting your elbows on the table and cupping your hands over your eyes. Take several slow, deep breaths to relax; uncover your eyes and slowly open them. Without moving your head, slowly raise your eyes towards the ceiling and inhale. Then lower your eyes to the floor and exhale, allowing the tension to flow out of your eyes and face. Repeat the raising and lowering movements twice, then again cup your hands over your eyes, close them and breathe deeply. Remove your hands and slowly open your eyes.

NIGHT BLINDNESS

Preventing Night Blindness. Night blindness (nyctalopia) is a condition where a person can see well in daylight but not in fading or dim light. Night blindness is often due to a deficiency of vitamin A.

Vitamin A Supplements. Night blindness can often be prevented by supplementing the diet with 2,500 to 7,500 IUs of vitamin A per day.

Heavy Drinkers. Heavy alcohol appears to interfere with the liver's ability to store and release vitamin A into the system. Heavy drinkers should consider supplementing their diet with vitamin A.

NOSE-BLEED

How To Stop. A nose-bleed occurs when a blood vessel in the inner lining of the nose breaks. Nose-bleeds are commonly due to breathing dry air for long periods, repeated blowing and injury. The following steps can help:

- While sitting up, pinch your nose between your thumb and forefinger. Pinch just hard enough to stop the bleeding but not enough to cause pain.
- Breathe slowly through your mouth as you continue to apply pressure for 5 minutes without interruption.
- If the bleeding doesn't stop, try again. After three attempts, get medical help.

NOSE DROPS

Best Way To Administer. Lie on your back and tilt your head backwards. Put the drops in each nostril. Remain in the same position until the medication has reached your sinuses. This should take about 2 to 4 minutes.

Clean the dropper with water and wipe with a tissue before placing it back in the bottle. This will prevent contamination.

ODOURS IN THE HOME

One Natural Way To Deodorise Your Home. Deodorisers and sprays available in supermarkets sometimes cause allergies. Try this natural way to rid your home of odours. Douse a few cotton balls in wintergreen oil. Place these cotton balls in the bathroom, kitchen and other rooms you want freshened.

OSTEOPOROSIS

Need For More Calcium. This is a condition where the bones become brittle and fracture easily due to loss of calcium. If allowed to progress, the spinal column may become curved due to body weight. The victim may also lose several inches in height. Osteoporosis is the cause of the 'hump back' look in so many older people.

Medical experts agree that most older women need more calcium in their diets. Some doctors are even recommending calcium supplements.

Daily Requirement. The recommended daily intake of calcium is 1,000 mg for adults. But experts say actual intake for adults is only 450 to 550 mg a day. Women who have passed menopause may need as much as 1,500 mg daily. Persons with a history of kidney-stones should consult a doctor before using calcium supplements.

Sources Of Calcium. Milk and other dairy products, fish, oranges and leafy green vegetables are major sources of calcium. A cup of skimmed milk has 300 to 350 mg.

Vitamin D is needed for optimum calcium absorption. The best time for women to take calcium supplements is at night, according to Dr Morris Notelovitz, Professor of Obstetrics and Gynaecology at the University of Florida. Foods rich in vitamin D include milk, salmon, tuna and sardines.

PAIN

Cold For Relief. Cold is the best remedy for the pain of injury, says Dr H Paul Bauer, Director of the Sports Therapy and Body Mechanics Clinic in San Diego, California. Applying ice will provide the following benefits:

- It numbs the affected area of pain.
- It decreases swelling by cutting down the blood supply.

Experts recommend leaving the ice on for 10 to 15 minutes at a time. Ice is preferred over heat for treating injuries such as sprains, bruises and torn muscles.

Pain And Tryptophan Research. Preliminary studies showed that L-tryptophan can help increase a person's tolerance to pain. L-tryptophan is an amino acid available in most health food shops.

The studies involved 30 subjects who were tested on their ability to tolerate pain with a device that sends jolts of electricity to the tooth pulp.

Fifteen of the subjects took 2 g of L-tryptophan daily for a week. The other 15 took a fake pill. When the subjects were retested at the end of the week, the 15 who had taken L-tryptophan were able to tolerate twice the pain as the 15 who had not taken the amino acid. Check with your own doctor before taking L-tryptophan, experts advise.

Another study published in Oral Surgery showed that patients who took L-tryptophan when having fillings experienced less pain than those taking a fake pill. Patients took 2 g of L-tryptophan spread out in 4 doses of 500 mg each.

Aspirin And Caffeine. You can accelerate the pain-relieving effect of aspirin by taking it with a cup of coffee, according to a study by Dr Bernard Schachtel at Yale University. In his study, aspirin taken with caffeine brought pain relief in 15 minutes.

PARKINSON'S DISEASE

Vitamins. Through research carried out at Columbia University it was found that the symptoms of Parkinson's Disease may be postponed by large, medically controlled doses of vitamins C and E. Patients tested managed without drug treatment for advanced Parkinson's symptoms for two and a half years longer than those not taking the vitamins. It is thought that because these vitamins neutralise tissue-damaging molecular fragments (free radicals) in the body.

Low-Protein Diet. L-dopa, a drug used to treat the symptoms of Parkinson's Disease, can be blocked as a result of a high-protein meal, says Dr Jonathan H Pincus, chairman of the Neurology Department at Georgetown University Medical Centre. He and other experts recommend that patients for whom L-dopa does not always work should stick to a low-protein diet during the day, and consume the required proteins in their evening meal, so that if L-dopa is blocked, it will occur while they are asleep.

PETS

Good Effects On People. A number of studies have shown that pets have a good effect on health. For example, according to a public health study, pet owners have a greater survival rate after heart attack. Other studies show that a dog can significantly lower blood pressure and reduce stress in children. Even fish and birds can have a beneficial effect on health. People tend to be more relaxed around pets. With a dog, people often feel safer.

Possible Bad Effects On People. Numerous diseases can be transmitted by pets. One common carrier of disease is dog faeces. According to a study conducted in Savannah, Georgia, a single deposit of dog faeces produced an average of 144 house flies. House flies may carry disease.

Dog bites are a nationwide problem. One person in every 250 in the United States is bitten annually.

PIMPLES

How To Stop Flareups.

When a pimple starts to become visible, apply ice for a few seconds every half hour. This should cause it to subside in a few hours. If it doesn't, apply a moist compress every hour.

To take the red out of a blemish, combine one tablespoon of lemon juice with one tablespoon of salt. Apply this mixture directly to the reddened area and leave it on for 10 minutes. Then rinse.

To get rid of a pimple overnight, dip a cotton wool bud in witch hazel and apply to the pimple to dry it up. Then apply calamine lotion.

POISONING, AVOIDING CHILD

Simple Precautionary Measures. Each year thousands of children are needlessly poisoned because adults do not take proper precautions to avoid accidental poisoning. A few simple steps can avoid a tragedy to a young child. Here are some valuable tips on 'poison proofing' your home.

• Keep handy the phone number of your local hospital.

- Know where poison antidotes are kept and how to use them.
- Keep medicines and household products out of children's sight and reach. If possible, lock them away.
- Safely discard prescription drugs no longer being taken.
- When purchasing prescription drugs, always make sure the containers are child-proof.
- When discussing medicines around children, never refer to them as sweets or something that should be casually eaten.
- Avoid taking any medicines in the presence of children.

Remember, always consult your doctor if you have any doubts at all.

PLASTERS, REMOVING

Taking The Sting Out. Removing plasters can be very painful, especially on children. The next time you have to remove a plaster, instead of ripping it off, try using a hair drier to heat it up. This will soften the adhesive and the plaster should peel off easily with little or no discomfort.

POTATOES

When To Avoid. Green potatoes contain a chemical called solanine that can cause brain and intestinal disorders, according to nutritional specialist, Carla Hughes of the University of Missouri, Columbia.

This poisonous ingredient cannot be boiled or fried away. Avoid the following:

- Potatoes that are green and bitter. Trim these affected areas away before eating.
- Avoid eating potato sprouts.
- Avoid potato stems that are green in colour.
- Always store potatoes in a dark place to avoid premature spoilage.

PREMENSTRUAL TENSION

Tips That May Help. Premenstrual tension is the nervousness and irritability experienced by some women the week before their period.

Other symptoms may include tiredness, depression, breast discomfort, temporary weight gain and bloating. Symptoms usually subside when the period starts. Experts estimate about 60% of women suffer premenstrual tension.

- Reduce salt intake two weeks before cycle starts. A research study showed that simply taking 50 mg of vitamin B-6 daily caused an overall improvement in symptoms in 63% of the women. Foods rich in vitamin B-6 include bananas, cabbage, green leafy vegetables, whole grains and fish.
- Taking calcium supplements may relieve premenstrual problems, according to preliminary studies at New York Medical College.

PRESCRIPTION DRUGS

Questions To Ask Your Doctor. The American Pharmaceutical Manufacturers' Association recommends that patients ask the following questions when their doctor gives them a prescription:

- What is the medicine's name and purpose?
- What results are expected from taking it?
- How long is it necessary to wait before reporting to the doctor if there are no changes in symptoms?
- Are there any side effects?
- What side effects, if any, are supposed to be reported to the doctor? (According to a recent survey most doctors don't fully explain side effects.)
- Are there any cautions to watch for when taking the medicine? Are there any foods or beverages to avoid? Other medications not to take? Any limitation on driving or other activities?
- How long should you use the medicine?
- Should you ask for a repeat prescription when you run out of the medication? Will you need to see the doctor before being given a repeat prescription?

PROSTATE TROUBLE

Man's Most Common Affliction. Prostate trouble is one of the most common afflictions of men. Medical authorities estimate that over half the men over the age of 45 suffer some kind of prostate symptoms. At age 80 or over, as many as 95% of men suffer prostate distress. Prostate troubles can cause a variety of symptoms such as frequency of urination, getting up nights to urinate, urgency, delay in starting, abnormal retention of urine, dribbling, pain and discomfort.

Benign Prostatic Hypertrophy (BPH). This is the most common prostate problem. Simply stated, BPH is an enlargement of the prostate gland that is not cancerous. The healthy prostate gland is about the size of a walnut. But enlarged, it can swell to the size of an orange. When the prostate becomes enlarged it can pinch the urethra tube causing a variety of prostate symptoms mentioned above.

Zinc And BPH Relief. Dr Irving Bush of Chicago's Cook County Hospital treated 19 patients who suffered from BPH. They received 34 mg of oral zinc a day for two months. After that they were placed on a long-term programme of zinc dosage between 11 and 23 mg a day. Of the 19 patients, all reported that their painful symptoms were relieved. Five of the patients showed a decrease in prostate size. Foods rich in zinc include seafood, spinach, mushrooms, whole grains and sunflower seeds.

Complete Voiding. Taking plenty of time to urinate when nature calls will ease the problem of getting up during the night, according to a report in the New England Journal of Medicine. Take plenty of time to empty the bladder - until nothing more comes out - but don't strain. Several weeks of this training may strengthen bladder control.

Cholesterol And BPH. Studies performed at Rutgers University showed a relationship between high-fat diets and BPH.

Another study reported to the American Urological Association showed that there may be a connection between high cholesterol levels and prostate disease.

A study at Metropolitan Hospital, New York, examined 100 prostates from men of all ages and found an 80% increase in cholesterol content of prostates with BPH. See the section under Cholesterol for ways to reduce cholesterol levels in your body.

Prostatitis. Prostatitis is an infection or inflammation of the prostate gland. Though not a serious disorder, prostatitis can be irritating and uncomfortable because it disrupts normal urination.

Zinc And Prostatitis Relief. Dr Irving Bush treated 200 patients with 11 to 34 mg oral zinc per day for up to 16 weeks. A relief of symptoms was reported by 70% of the patients. All 200 patients registered higher zinc levels. Other studies have shown that zinc has a bacteria-killing effect on the bacteria most often associated with prostate infection.

Dr Warren Heston, PhD, Assistant Professor of Urology at the Washington University School of Medicine in St Louis, reported that prostatic fluid of men having prostatitis had only about one tenth the zinc of men free of this prostate trouble. Foods rich in zinc include seafood, spinach, mushrooms, whole grains and sunflower seeds.

Overall Prostate Health. A ten year study covering 122,261 men aged 40 and over showed that men with a low intake of green and yellow vegetables suffered prostate cancer twice as much as those men who ate plenty of vegetables. This link between green and yellow vegetables and prostate cancer was observed in every age group, social class and region study. Scientists speculated that green and yellow vegetables are rich in vitamin A which may be responsible for the lower rate of prostate cancer.

PSORIASIS

5 Tips That May Help. Psoriasis is a skin disease producing thick red eruptions on the arms, legs or head. In severe cases it can spread throughout the entire body. Psoriasis has been evident since Biblical times. There is no known cure and it also reacts eratically to treatment. One medication may help one and have no effect on others. Therefore sufferers should be prepared to try all the therapies available until they find the one that best suits them. The following measures often help:

● *Clean.* Cleaning the skin is important to help prevent infection. Lotions and creams available at chemists can cleanse and reduce itching. Many of these preparations contain coal tar that helps remove scales.

- *Sun.* Many people find that regular exposure to the sun is helpful. Where sunlight is scarce a sun lamp is often used with a doctor's supervision.
- *Gluten.* French researchers have found a link between psoriasis and problems in digesting gluten - a protein found in grain such as oats, barley, rye and wheat. In a preliminary study, 11 people with severe psoriasis were given a gluten-free diet. This gluten-free diet helped them greatly.
- *Fish Oil.* Some preliminary research has shown that Omega-3 fish oil may bring significant relief from the redness, scaling and skin crustations associated with psoriasis. However, many experts believe fish oil will only bring relief when combined with conventional medication. Fish oil supplements should not be taken without medical supervision, as long-term effects can be harmful.

  A British study at the Royal Hallamshire Hospital in Sheffield also found fish oil to be effective, using the equivalent of 5.5 oz of mackerel per day. Sardines and salmon are also good sources of Omega-3 fish oil.
- *Tar Ointments.* These treatments are safe and cheap, but can be very messy. Including crude coal tar and anthralin, they must be applied daily and kept on for at least half an hour and possibly several hours, depending on the severity of the case.

PULSE RATE

Checking Your Pulse Rate. A normal pulse rate for an adult is between 62 and 72 beats per minute when at rest. Normal pulse rate for children varies with age. The average pulse rate for a new born infant is about 120 beats per minute. A child's pulse rate can be anywhere from 60 to 90 beats per minute. An older child should have an average pulse rate of about 80. Normal pulse rates increase with activity, excitement and other factors.

The proper way to take a pulse is to place the index finger lightly on the radial artery at the wrist and count the beats for a full minute. Do not use the thumb to take the pulse rate. It may result in an inaccurate reading because the thumb has a pulse of its own.

RECTAL ITCHING

Suggestions To Relieve Itch. After each bowel movement take these four steps.

1. Cleanse the rectal area with soap and warm water. Rinse away the soap thoroughly. This procedure is much less irritating than tissue paper.
2. Sponge off the entire rectal area with rubbing alcohol. This helps kill germs and helps dry the skin.
3. Gently powder the area with talcum powder or corn starch. Powder helps the skin resist itch-producing fluids which may seep from the rectum.
4. Take a wad of cotton wool about half the size of a cigarette. Sprinkle it with talcum powder or corn starch. Place this cotton about half an inch into the rectal opening - just far enough so that it will stay in place. This will soak up any seepage. If large haemorrhoids are present you may need to make the piece of cotton wool larger.

RELAXATION

May Increase Immunity To Disease. A study performed at Ohio University showed that relaxation can cut down on stress and increase resistance to disease. Relaxation increases disease-fighting agents in the blood. These have the effect of bolstering the immune system against disease. Stress has the opposite effect on the body.

Simple Way To Relax. Close your eyes and breathe in slowly. As you inhale, say to yourself - I AM. Then exhale slowly saying - RELAXED. Feel your entire body loosen up and become free of tension. Repeat until you feel more relaxed.

RESISTANCE TO DISEASE

Older Persons And Zinc. Supplementing the diet with zinc may help the elderly increase resistance to disease, according to the results of a study by researchers at the University of California, San Diego, School of Medicine, and VA Medical Centre in La Jolla, California. The study found that the equivalent of 100 mg of zinc a day doubled the number of antibody-producing cells in subjects whose ages ranged from 66 to 85. Antibodies are generally considered the body's first line of defence against disease.

The recommended daily requirement of zinc is 15 mg per day. Foods rich in zinc include seafood, spinach, mushrooms, whole grains and sunflower seeds.

General Strengthening Of Immune System. Other nutrients which can naturally strengthen the immune system are vitamin A, beta-carotene, vitamin C, vitamin E, selenium and the amino acid called L-cysteine.

REYES' SYNDROME

Preventing Problems. Reyes' Syndrome is a rare but often fatal disease that may follow flu or chicken pox. It occurs mostly in younger children but can also affect teenagers.

Reyes' Syndrome often strikes when the flu or chicken pox victim seems to be recovering. The symptoms include violent headache, persistent vomiting, lethargy and sleepiness, beligerence, disorientation and delirium.

Reyes' Syndrome And Aspirin - A Possible Link. The cause of Reyes' Syndrome is not known but some studies suggest a possible link with the use of aspirin in flu or chicken pox. Manufacturers of aspirin in America are now voluntarily putting a warning on labels which says that a doctor should be consulted before aspirin is given to children, including teenagers, who have flu or chicken pox.

As a parent, if you feel you must do something while your child has either of these illnesses, check with your doctor to see what he recommends.

ROMANCE

2 Key Ways Women Start Romances. Romance can be good for your mental health. It can reduce stress and promote relaxation. Women start almost all romances, says researcher Dr Heather Remoff. They use two main ways of initiating a romance.

- The woman arranges to be near a man. For example, at work she could arrange to be by a man during a coffee break or the lunch hour.
- Women also use signals to let men know they are interested in them. These signals can take the form of fluttering of the eye lids and movements of the body.

SALT

Cutting Down On Your Intake. The medical world is recommending reducing salt intake for better health. Here are some ways to do it:

- *Salt Shaker.* Researchers at the University of New South Wales in Sydney, Australia studied over 2,000 diners using salt shakers with holes of various sizes. The study showed that persons using the shakers with smaller holes used less salt.
- *Lemon Juice As Salt.* A research study published in the Journal of the American Dietetic Association indicacted that volunteers could not tell the difference between tomato juice seasoned with lemon juice (or citric acid) and salt.
- *Herbs As Salt.* Try replacing salt with a blend of herbs. Combine oregano, onion powder, garlic, basil, bay leaf and pepper.

SECOND OPINION (SURGERY)

Doctors sometimes have differing opinions about medical problems. One doctor may recommend surgery. Another may tell you to wait. Another may recommend some other form of treatment. When you get a second opinion you get more information and increase your chances of making the right decision.

Questions You Should Ask.
1. What does the doctor say is the matter with you?
2. What is the operation the doctor plans to do?
3. What are the likely benefits to you of the operation?
4. What are the risks of the surgery and how likely are they to occur?
5. How long would the recovery period be and what is involved?

6. If you are having the operation done privately, what are the costs and will your insurance cover all of those costs?
7. What will happen if you don't have the operation?
8. Are there other ways to treat your condition that could be tried first?

SHINGLES

Speeding Up Relief. Shingles is an outbreak of blisters on reddened skin. It is a highly painful condition. Shingles is caused by the same virus that causes chicken pox. It generally strikes persons over 50. One shingles attack usually gives the victim immunity against another attack.

- *Vitamin E.* A study published in Archives of Dermatology showed that patients who received about 400 mg daily of vitamin E and who applied vitamin E to the sores directly showed an improvement in their condition.
- *Vitamin B-12 And C.* Some shingles sufferers have reported some success by taking large doses of vitamin B-12. Others report supplements of vitamin C helped overcome this condition.

SINUS CONGESTION

Suggestions For Preventing Flareups. Sinus congestion is due to an inflammation of the mucous membranes that line sinus cavities. It can be triggered by anything that prevents mucus from draining properly. Possibilities include allergies, colds or flu, abscessed teeth, emotional stress, swimming and diving without nose plugs. Sinus congestion is often caused by a bacterial infection in the sinus cavities. Common symptoms are headache and tenderness in the forehead above and behind the eyes. Here are some rules to follow to avoid problems:

- Avoid substances you're allergic to.
- Avoid abrupt temperature changes, for example, wear a sweater in an air-conditioned room and dress warmly when you go outside on a cold day.
- Avoid household aerosol sprays. They can trigger a sinus attack. Also avoid scented soaps, tissue paper and perfumes.

- Smoke can trigger a sinus problem. Avoid smoky rooms. Keep your oven clean. Also keep burners clean. They can send smoke throughout the house.
- Have regular dental check-ups. Tooth infections can easily spread into the sinuses causing problems.

3 Tips For Relieving Sinus Congestion.
- Inhale steam from a vapouriser, especially in dry climates.
- Apply an ice pack to the bridge of the nose and across the cheek bones. This shrinks inflamed tissues.
- When sinus congestion is caused by sinusitis, a bacterial infection, you should visit your doctor for treatment.

Salt Water For Sinus Congestion. To relieve sinus congestion thoroughly dissolve one rounded teaspoon of table salt into one pint of warm, distilled water. (Using distilled water is important. Tap water contains chlorine and other chemicals which may be irritating to sinuses.) Cup the solution into the palm of your hand. Hold it to the nose and breathe in. Tip the head backwards so the solution can be drawn into the throat, then spit out the solution.

Vitamin A. An article published in Nutritional Support of Medical Practice indicates that vitamin A may actually thin mucous membranes. A lack of vitamin A may contribute to sinus congestion by hardening the membranes. Even a minor deficiency may trigger problems. Vitamin A is responsible for production of mucus-producing cells. Foods rich in vitamin A include broccoli, carrots, fish, green and yellow fruits and low-fat milk.

Heat And Water. To clear sinus congestion apply hot towels to sinus area for 1 or 2 hours, 4 times a day, says Dr Bryon Baily from Galveston, Texas. Also, drink plenty of water to clear out congestion.

Massaging Away Sinus Headache. Massaging the temple and forehead above the eyes will help relax facial nerves. This relieves tightly drawn areas of the face and brings relief to sinus and eye discomfort, according to Dr L L Schneider, author of "Old-Fashioned Health Remedies".

SKIN

Tips For General Care. The skin is the largest body organ covering and protecting tissues, bones and organs. The skin is exposed - it's first to take abuse from the outside world. Because of this, it is subject to many disorders. The skin reveals the age of the body. Sometimes the skin becomes dry and rough due to a deficiency of vitamin A. The result is that the small bumps at the base of hair follicles become hardened; this condition is known as folliculosis.

The following recommendations will help keep skin youthful:

• Avoid harsh soaps and abrasive cleansers.
• Use a good moisturiser regularly.
• Avoid facial exercises, they stretch the skin. That can cause wrinkles. The less you move your face the better.
• Avoid going in the sun as much as possible, especially the midday sun.
• If you cannot avoid being in the sun, use a sun screen. The sun can damage your skin permanently. A severe skin burn may take 15 or 20 years to show up. That's when wrinkles and sagging skin start.
• Avoid smoking. Cigarette smoke destroys the small blood vessels in your skin which causes it to age.
• For oily skin use toners and astringents. Use during the day whenever skin gets too oily.
• Never use toners or astringents on dry skin.
• Use a hat or visor to block out the sun's rays. This is especially important with sensitive skin.

Keep Skin Healthy In The Winter. Winters are particularly harsh on your skin. Cold weather outside affects skin one way and heating conditions inside another. Here are some tips for winter skin care:

• Drink at least 6 glasses of liquid a day.
• Use a skin protector plus a moisturiser. One of the best protectors found in many skin care products is dimethicone. The best moisturiser is urea and a glyul compound. Also, use a moisturiser for your lips.
• Dampen and tone your skin twice a day.

- Properly care for hidden areas of your skin like elbows and heels. Cleanse with a gentle scrub once a week. Then apply a moisturising cream.
- Don't forget about caring for your throat and upper chest. These areas usually get the same exposure as the face.
- Avoid extreme changes in temperature. Before coming indoors, stop and take a minute to warm your cheeks and nose with your hands. This will help avoid risk of broken capillaries caused by abrupt temperature changes.

SLEEP

Tips For Getting A Good Night's Sleep.
- Drink a mug of warm milk before going to bed.
- A warm bath or shower helps induce relaxation. Taking a warm bath or shower has the opposite effect of taking a cold shower to wake you up in the morning.
- Avoid drinking coffee or any other stimulants several hours before retiring.
- Reduce salt intake. One research study showed high salt intake interfered with normal sleep.
- Avoid alcohol before bedtime. Studies show alcohol interferes with normal sleep cycles. It also depresses normal dream cycles.
- Go to bed only when tired. If you don't fall asleep in a short while, get up again until you feel tired.

Relieving Tension Before Bed. Tension is a common cause of insomnia. You have a better chance of getting a good night's sleep if you can relieve tension. This simple exercise can help.

- Reach as high as possible.
- Hold this position while standing on tip-toes with fingers outreached as if reaching for the ceiling. Count to 30.
- Let go. Shake the arms and legs. Then retire and enjoy a good night's sleep. (Repeat exercise if necessary.)

Sleep and Valerian. Sleep researchers at the Nestle Research Laboratories in La Tour-de-Peilz, Switzerland, serve steaming cups of that age-old sleep inducer Valerian. British doctors during World War II used tinctures of this herb to calm the shattered nerves of bombing-raid victims. In a recent study of 128 sleep-troubled men and women, Valerian produced significant improvements in sleep quality. Improvements were most notable among poor or irregular sleepers. Valerian does not affect dream recall or cause morning-after drowsiness, the way some prescription sleeping pills and over-the-counter sleep aids do.

Copper And Iron. A deficiency in copper and iron could be a cause of sleep trouble in women, according to research by the US Department of Agriculture. It was found that women on an iron-deficient diet had 20% more awakenings during the night than those with a normal iron intake. Women on a low-copper diet took 10% longer to fall asleep and experienced a lower quality of sleep than those consuming adequate copper. If you think either of these deficiencies may be your problem, then supplements should be taken on your doctor's advice.

SMOKING

Greater Heart Attack Risks For Women. Smoking is associated with heart disease, cancer, emphysema and other ailments. Women under 50 who smoke heavily are seven times more likely to have a heart attack than non-smokers. When taking the birth control pill they have an even higher risk of heart attack.

Depletion Of Vitamin C. Every cigarette depletes the body of about 25 mg of vitamin C. Some researchers say that heavy smokers need at least 140 mg of vitamin C a day.

What Happens When You Quit. The moment you quit smoking your body starts to benefit, according to the American Cancer Society.

- Within 20 minutes your blood pressure and pulse rate drop to normal, and oxygen level of blood increases to normal.
- After 24 hours your chance of heart attack decreases.
- After 48 hours your ability to smell and taste improves.
- After 72 hours bronchial tubes relax, making breathing easier. Lung capacity also increases.

- After 2 weeks to 3 months your circulation improves and lung function increases up to 30%.
- From 1 to 9 months after quitting coughing, sinus congestion, fatigue and shortness of breath decrease. Your overall body energy level increases.
- After 5 years lung cancer death rate decreases. (Tobacco contains 30 cancer-causing agents.)
- After 10 years lung cancer death rate drops to 12 deaths per 100,000 - almost the same rate as non-smokers. Pre-cancerous cells are replaced. The risk of other cancers such as mouth, larynx, oesophagus, bladder, kidney and pancreas also decreases.

14 Suggestions For Cutting Down On Cigarette Smoking. The American National Cancer Institute recommends the following:

- Smoke only half of each cigarette.
- Each day, postpone lighting your first cigarette one hour.
- Decide you will smoke only during odd or even hours of the day.
- Decide beforehand how many cigarettes you'll smoke during the day. For each additional smoke, give a pound to your favourite charity. Don't smoke when you first experience a craving. Wait several minutes; and during this time, change your activity or talk to someone.
- Stop buying more than one packet of cigarettes at a time; wait until one packet is empty before buying another.
- Stop carrying cigarettes with you at home and at work. Make them difficult to get to.
- Smoke only under circumstances which are not particularly enjoyable for you. If you like to smoke with others, smoke alone.
- Make yourself aware of each cigarette by using the opposite hand, or putting cigarettes in an unfamiliar location or different pocket to break the automatic reach.
- If you light up many times during the day without even thinking about it, try to look in a mirror each time you put a match to your cigarette - you may decide you don't need it.
- Don't smoke 'automatically'. Smoke only those you really want.
- Reward yourself in some way other than smoking.
- Reach for a glass of juice instead of a cigarette for a 'pick-me-up'.

- Change your eating habits to aid in cutting down. For example, drink milk, which is frequently considered incompatible with smoking. End meals or snacks with something which won't lead to a cigarette.
- Don't empty your ashtrays. This will not only remind you of how many cigarettes you have smoked each day, but the sight and smell of stale butts will be very unpleasant.

Quitting Smoking - The First Day. On the day you decide to quit smoking do the following, says the American National Cancer Institute:

- Throw away all cigarettes and matches. Hide lighters and ashtrays.
- Visit the dentist and have your teeth cleaned to get rid of tobacco stains. Notice how nice they look and resolve to keep them that way.
- Make a list of things you'd like to buy yourself or someone else. Estimate the cost in terms of packs of cigarettes, and put the money aside to buy these presents.
- Keep very busy on the big day. Go to the cinema, exercise, take long walks, go cycling.
- Buy yourself a treat or do something to celebrate.

Immediately After Quitting.
- The first few days after you quit, spend as much free time as possible in places where smoking is not permitted, eg. libraries, museums, theatres, department stores, churches.
- Drink large quantities of water and fruit juice.
- Try to avoid alcohol, coffee and other beverages with which you associate cigarette smoking.
- Strike up a conversation with someone instead of a match for a cigarette.
- If you miss the sensation of having a cigarette in your hand, play with something else - a pencil, a paper clip, a marble.
- If you miss having something in your mouth, try toothpicks or a fake cigarette.

Avoid Temptation.
- Instead of smoking after meals, get up from the table and brush your teeth or go for a walk.
- If you always smoke while driving, use public transport for a time.

- Temporarily avoid situations you strongly associate with the pleasurable aspects of smoking, eg. watching your favourite television programme, sitting in your favourite chair, having a cocktail before dinner.
- Develop a clean, fresh, non-smoking environment around yourself - at work and at home.
- Until you are confident of your ability to stay off cigarettes, limit your socialising to healthy, outdoor activities or situations where smoking is prohibited. If you must be in a situation where you will be tempted to smoke (such as a cocktail or dinner party), try to associate with the non-smokers there.
- Look at cigarette adverts more critically so you see through the attempt to make individual brands appealing.

When You Have The Urge.
- Keep oral substitutes handy - things like carrots, pickles, sunflower seeds, apples, celery, raisins, chewing gum and so on.
- Take ten deep breaths and hold the last one while lighting a match. Exhale slowly and blow out the match. Pretend it is a cigarette and crush it out in an ashtray.
- Take a shower or bath if possible.
- Learn to relax quickly and deeply. Make yourself limp, visualising a soothing, pleasing situation and get away from it all for a moment. Concentrate on that peaceful image and nothing else.
- Light incense or a candle instead of a cigarette.

SNEEZING

Don't Hold Back A Sneeze. Sneezing releases bacteria and viruses that can prolong your illness. Holding back a sneeze may infect your sinuses and even cause ear infection, says Dr Chole, Professor at the University of California. When you sneeze you should sneeze with your mouth open but covered with your hand.

SNORING

4 Suggestions For Snorers.
- Sleep on your side rather than on your back. Prop pillows either side of your body to prevent rolling over on your back.
- Avoid tranquillisers or sleeping pills.
- Tilt the bed with the head upwards. The best way is to put 6 to 8 inch wooden blocks under the front legs of the bed.
- Avoid alcoholic beverages within 2 hours of going to bed.

STIFF NECK

Relieving Discomfort. Stiff necks are most often caused by a muscle cramp brought about by a chill, sleeping in a cramped position or sudden twisting movement, for example when reversing a car. Try these suggestions for fast relief:

- Apply hot packs, or take a hot shower concentrating on the sore neck area.
- Gently massage neck. A vibrator is often helpful.
- Take aspirin or paracetamol to relieve pain if needed.

Stiff Neck Exercise.
1. While standing, let the head move slowly forward and downward without forcing it.
2. Firmly interlace the fingers behind the neck.
3. Slowly bring the head upwards as if to look at the ceiling directly above. Hold the head in this position for approximately 30 seconds.
4. Relax to normal position resting 2 or 3 minutes.
5. Repeat the same procedure six times starting with step 1 and resting after each stretching.

Stiff Neck Rub. Use a solution of 15% oil of wintergreen and 85% rubbing alcohol. Apply this solution to the stiff muscles of your neck. Rub very lightly. After the area is well coated cover it with a hot damp cloth, recommends Dr L L Schneider, author of "Old-Fashioned Health Remedies".

STRESS

How To Deal With Stress. Stress is with us all the time. It is an unavoidable part of our lives. Stress is unique and personal to each of us. What may be stressful to one person may actually be relaxing to another. Stress can be defined as too much of the wrong sort of pressure. Too much emotional stress can cause physical illness such as high blood pressure, ulcers or even heart disease. Recognising early signs of stress and then doing something about it can make an important difference in the quality of your life. It may actually influence your survival.

How The Body Reacts To Stress. To use stress in a positive way and prevent it from becoming distress, you should make yourself aware of your own reactions to stressful events. The body responds to stress by going through three stages: (1) alarm, (2) recovery and (3) exhaustion.

Let's take the example of a typical commuter in rush-hour traffic. If a car suddenly pulls out in front of him, his initial alarm reaction may include fear of an accident, anger at the driver who committed the action and general frustration. His body may respond to the alarm stage by releasing hormones into the bloodstream which cause his face to flush, perspiration to form, his stomach to have a sinking feeling and his arms and legs to tighten. The next stage is recovery, in which the body repairs damage caused by the stress. If the stress of driving continues with repeated close calls or traffic jams, however, his body will not have time to make repairs. He may become so conditioned to accept potential problems when he drives that he tightens up at the beginning of each commuting day. Eventually, he may develop one of the diseases of stress, such as migraine headaches, high blood pressure, backaches or insomnia. While it is impossible to live completely free of stress and distress, it is possible to prevent some distress as well as to minimise its impact when it can't be avoided.

Helping Yourself. When stress does occur, it is important to recognise and deal with it. Here are some suggestions. As you begin to understand more about how stress affects you as an individual, you will come up with your own ideas of helping to ease the tensions.

- *Try Physical Activity.* When you are nervous, angry or upset, release the pressures through exercise or physical activity. Running, walking or playing tennis or working in your garden are just some of the activities you may try. Physical exercise will relieve that 'up-tight' feeling, relax you and turn frowns into smiles. Remember, your body and your mind work together.

- *Share Your Stress.* It helps to talk to someone about your concerns and worries. Perhaps a friend, family member, teacher or counsellor can help you see your problem in a different light. If you feel your problem is serious, you might seek professional help from a psychologist, psychiatrist or social worker. Knowing when to ask for help may avoid more serious problems later.

- *Know Your Limits.* If a problem is beyond your control and cannot be changed at the moment, don't fight the situation. Learn to accept what is - for now - until such time as when you can change it. Learn how to say no to demands that overburden you.

- *Take Care Of Yourself.* You are special. Get enough rest and eat well. If you are irritable and tense from lack of sleep or if you are not eating correctly, you will have less ability to deal with stressful situations. If stress repeatedly keeps you from sleeping, you should ask your doctor for help.

- *Train Yourself To Stop Worrying.* Banish your worries by doing something about the situation. If you can't do anything about it then there's no point in wasting time thinking about it. Make sure you don't start feeling guilty for not worrying.

- *Make Time For Fun.* Schedule time for both work and recreation. Play can be just as important to your well-being as work; you need a break from your daily routine just to relax and have fun.

- *Be A Participant.* One way to keep from getting bored and lonely is to go to where it's all happening. Sitting alone can make you feel frustrated. Instead of feeling sorry for yourself, get involved and become a participant. Offer your services to local charities. Help yourself by helping other people. Get involved in the world and the people around you and you will find they'll be attracted to you. You're on the way to making new friends and enjoying new activities.

- *Tick Off Your Tasks.* Trying to take care of everything at once can seem overwhelming and, as a result, you may not accomplish anything. Instead, make a list of what tasks you have to do, then do one at a time, ticking them off as they're completed. Give priority to the most important tasks and do those first.

- **Must You Always Be Right?** Do other people upset you - particularly when they don't do things your way? Try co-operation instead of confrontation; it's better than fighting and always being 'right'. A little give and take on both sides will reduce the strain and make you both feel more comfortable.
- **It's Okay To Cry.** A good cry can be a healthy way to bring relief to your anxiety and it may even prevent a headache or other physical consequence. Take some deep breaths; they also help relieve tension.
- **Laughter.** Laughter can also make you feel much better - try to look at the bright side of life.
- **Create A Quiet Scene.** You can't always run away, but you can 'dream the impossible dream'. A quiet country scene painted mentally, or on canvas, can take you out of the turmoil of a stressful situation. Change the scene by reading a good book or playing beautiful music to create a sense of peace and tranquillity.
- **Avoid Medication.** Although you can use drugs to relieve stress temporarily, drugs do not remove the conditions that have caused the stress in the first place. Drugs, in fact, may be habit-forming and create more stress than they take away. They should be taken only on the advice of your doctor.

The Art Of Relaxation. The best strategy for avoiding stress is to learn how to relax. Unfortunately, many people try to relax at the same pace that they lead the rest of their lives. For a while, tune out of your worries about time, productivity and 'doing right'. You will find satisfaction in just being, without striving. Find activities that give you pleasure and that are good for your mental and physical well-being. Forget about always winning. Focus on relaxation, enjoyment and health. Be good to yourself.

Nutritional Considerations. Excessive amounts of stress can deplete your body of essential nutrients, thereby weakening your coping abilities.

- **B-Complex Vitamins.** B-complex vitamins help maintain the health of your nervous system. Even a slight vitamin B deficiency can cause irritability and depression.
- **Vitamin B-1** (Thiamin). Several dietary factors interfere with the ability of your body to utilise thiamin. Consuming sugar raises thiamin requirements.

Thiamin is affected by tannic acid, so the consumption of 4 to 6 cups of tea per day can cause symptomatic thiamin deficiency. Also, heavy alcohol consumption is known for its ability to cause a thiamin deficiency, according to a study in Nutritional Abborations and Clinical Pharmacy and Therapeutics.

- *Pantothenic Acid.* Pantothenic acid is another B-vitamin that can improve the ability of even well-nourished people to withstand stress.
- *Vitamin C.* During times of physical stress vitamin C needs are higher than the recommended dietary allowance. Also, infections, burns and cigarette smoking drain the tissues of vitamin C.
- *Magnesium.* Magnesium is another nutrient drained from the body by stress. Studies indicate that a magnesium deficiency weakens the body's ability to cope with stress.

When the body is not provided with complete nutrition it is more difficult for it to recover from the physical effects of stress.

STRETCH MARKS

Try Vitamin E. Many people have reported that vitamin E cream helps soften and relieve stretch marks. Also, supplementing the diet with about 400 IUs of vitamin E daily helps stretch marks. Foods rich in vitamin E include dark green vegetables, fruits and rice.

STROKES

Potassium In Your Diet. Researchers at Cambridge University School of Medicine and the University of California at San Diego School of Medicine conducted a study over 12 years into the relationship between diet and strokes. They found that no stroke deaths occurred among those who consumed the highest levels of potassium. To reduce your risk of death by stroke by 40%, simply eat one extra serving each day of a potassium-rich food, such as baked potatoes, bananas, orange juice, tomato juice, tinned sardines and avocados.

STUTTERING

Help Is Available. Many famous people throughout history have stuttered. They include Moses, Winston Churchill, King George VI, Charles Darwin, Thomas Jefferson and James Stewart. Experts say that stutterers are cleverer than the average person, having an IQ about 14 points higher. Stutterers can be cured or helped considerably to control the problem. Most of the therapies involve concentration on air flow to the vocal chords and relaxing. By doing this trigger muscular spasms often responsible for stuttering. Hypnosis proved to be a highly effective therapy for stuttering.

SUGAR

4 Reasons To Cut Sugar Intake. Many experts are recommending reduced intake of refined sugar. Here are some reasons why:

- High intake of sugar can deplete the body's supply of B vitamins, particularly vitamin B-1. This can result in poor concentration, memory problems, irritability and depression.
- Sugar produces a short-term energy boost lasting about one hour. After that the energy level plummets.
- Sugar may be habit forming. It increases the production of insulin resulting in lower blood sugar levels. This can lead to a strong craving for sugar on a continual basis.
- Sugar also promotes tooth decay. The more sugar you consume, the higher your chances of developing cavities.

Sugar Substitutes. Instead of sprinkling sugar over cereal or fruit, try a blend of sweet spices, such as cinnamon, nutmeg, cloves, allspice and aniseed.

SUNTAN

Suggestions For Preventing Skin Damage. A suntan makes you look great, but beware of the longer-term effects. Over time the sun's rays will leave your skin tough, leathery and dry, say skin experts. Crow's-feet around

the eyes are often caused by sq_____ _____ _____ right sunlight. Prevent damage
to your skin by following som_ _____ _____ _____

- Avoid peak hours of sunshine between _____ am and 2 pm. This is when
  ultraviolet rays are at their stro____st.
- Limit your exposure to the sun. Depending _ your type of skin, you should
  begin with only 15 _____s in ___ ___n. U_ _unta__ otions that contain sun
  screen. Sun screen _ange fr_ _____ __ngth _n 2 to __. These Sun Protection
  Factors (SPFs) give you ___ _____ _____ stay in the sun without
  burning. For exampl_, ___ _____ _____ the sun for 15 minutes
  without burning, a lot_ _____ _____ _____ _ould allow you to stay in the
  sun for 30 minutes. _ _____ __ing of the various sun protection
  factors.

  1. SPF 2 to 4: Minimal protection from s_ ___ning. Perm__ _ suntanning.
     Recommended for people who rarely bur_ __d tan easily.
  2. SPF 4 to 6: Moderate protection from _unb__ __i_g. Pe_ __ _ome
     suntanning. Recommended for peopl_ _ ho ___ with _ _ima_ _ _ing.
  3. SPF 6 to 8: Extra protection from sunbu _n..g. Permits _ _ited su___ _
     ning. Recommended for people wh_ _ur_ _oderately a_ _____ du__ _
  4. SPF 8 to under 15: Maximum protectio_ __ _n sunbu__i_ _r_in _ittl_
     or no suntanning. Recommended for people who burn easily a__ tan
     minimally.
  5. SPF 15 or greater: Ultra protection from sunburn. Permits no suntan-
     ning. Recommended for people who burn easily and never tan.
- Apply lotion all over your body. Make sure you have enough lotion on
  sensitive areas such as nose, lips and shoulders.
- Try to avoid squinting while in the sun. The tiny lines around your ey_
  commonly called 'crow's-feet' can be caused by squinting.
- Remember that the sun's rays penetrate water about 3 ft below the surfac_
  So don't think you are not being exposed to the sun because you're und_
  water.
- In high altitudes air is less dense and burning rays are more intense. This
  means you are more likely to burn.
- When you've had enough sun but are not ready to leave, cover up with
  clothing. That will block out the sun's rays.

- After exposure to the sun take a warm shower, then smooth on a moisturising cream or lotion.

SWALLOWING PILLS AND CAPSULES

The Best Way To Swallow.
- *Tablets.* A tablet should be placed in the mouth with a small amount of water. The head should be tilted backwards and the tablet or pill swallowed, says Dr Ace Brown of Doctor's Hospital in Augusta, Georgia.
- *Capsules.* A capsule should be placed in your mouth with a small sip of water. Then tip your head or upper part of your body forward. This will cause the capsule to float towards the back of the mouth where it can be swallowed easily.

TEETH, SENSITIVE

The Cause. About 1 in every 4 adults experience the painful discomfort of sensitive teeth. This can occur when the natural protective tooth covering wears away or when the gums surrounding the root of the tooth recede. As a result, the root surface becomes exposed making it extra sensitive to heat and cold, causing discomfort and pain.

Toothpaste For Sensitive Teeth. Special toothpaste is now available for people with sensitive teeth. To obtain maximum relief it is important to brush at least twice a day or as your dentist directs. If you brush infrequently or stop brushing once the pain is reduced, sensitivity could return.

TEETH AND GUMS

3 Tips To Keep Them Healthy.
- Use a fluoride toothpaste.
- Use unwaxed dental floss between teeth and below gum line.
- Use a water irrigating device to stimulate and thoroughly clean your gums, according to the American Dental Association.

TEMPERATURE

Finding Your Normal Temperature. The body temperature for a normal adult is 98.6°F when the thermometer is placed under the tongue. When the temperature is taken through the rectum, it is about 1 degree higher.

Temperatures can vary from 98.6°F and still be normal. To find out your normal temperature, take it when you are feeling well. The next time you are sick you can measure the variation from normal.

Oral Temperature. Oral temperature should not be taken after you have had a cold drink or brushed your teeth. Wait 15 to 30 minutes. Then follow these basic steps:

1. Wash your hands and rinse the thermometer in cool water.
2. Holding the thermometer by the top (not the bulb end) shake it with a quick snap of the wrist until the mercury goes down to 96°F or lower.
3. Place the bulb end of the thermometer well under the tongue and keep the mouth closed (without biting) for at least 3 minutes. Young children and elderly patients should not be left alone with a fever thermometer in place.
4. Remove the thermometer and rotate it until the mercury lever can be seen. A good light helps but don't hold the thermometer close to a lamp. The heat could affect the reading.

Rectal Temperature. Follow these basic steps:
1. Wash your hands and rinse the thermometer in cool water.
2. Holding the thermometer by the top, shake it with a quick snap of the wrist until the mercury goes down to 96°F or lower.
3. Lubricate the thermometer with, for example, petroleum jelly.
4. Have the patient lie on one side and breathe through the mouth. Infants and small children may be on their sides, backs or tummies. Separate the buttocks with your free hand and gently insert the thermometer almost half an inch into the rectum. Leave it, or hold it in place, especially in infants and toddlers, for about 4 minutes.
5. Remove, wipe off the lubricant and read it like an oral thermometer. Rectal temperatures are about 1 degree higher than oral readings.

6. After use. wash the thermometer in cool, soapy water. Never wash in warm or hot water and do not store near heat.

TENDONITIS

Suggestions For Relief Of Tendonitis Discomfort. Tendonitis is an inflammation of the tissues that connect muscles to the bone. It is common in people over 30 and can be caused by sudden stress or prolonged activity. It most often affects the hand, shoulder, ankle, knee or hip.

- Give the affected area a period of rest until pain subsides.
- Apply ice to the affected area three or four times a day for periods up to 20 minutes.
- After about two days replace the ice treatments with heat treatments. The heat treatments can be hot packs, heating pads or hot showers.

Preventing Tendonitis. Taking time to warm up before physical activity is a simple way to prevent tendonitis, For example, calf and leg muscle stretching before jogging may help prevent tendonitis in the Achilles' tendon.

TENSION

Suggestions To Help You Relax.
- Sit quietly in a comfortable position.
- Close your eyes.
- Relax all your muscles beginning at your feet and progressing up to your face.
- Do this twice daily.

Quick Tension-Relief Method. Your eyes use a quarter of the nervous energy consumed by the body, says Dr Edmund Jacobson of the University of Chicago. Relaxing the eyes can help relax the entire body.

Try this simple, quick method. Lean back and close your eyes. Then silently tell your eyes let go. Stop frowning. Stop straining. Let go. Let go. Repeat for at least 1 minute.

THROAT, SORE

5 Tips To Reduce Discomfort.
- Gargle with warm salt water every 2 hours for about 5 minutes (1 teaspoon salt per 8 oz glass of warm water).
- Drink plenty of water or juices (about 8 oz per hour).
- Take aspirin or paracetamol for mild fever and discomfort.
- Suck lozenges to help relieve pain.
- Don't smoke or stay in a smoky room.

When To Call The Doctor.
- Sore throat continues for 5 days.
- Fever over 101°F.
- Rash develops.
- You have history of rheumatic fever or kidney disease.

Your Toothbrush. A study in Medical World News reported that bacteria living on your toothbrush can cause lingering throat infections. It takes only 17 to 35 days for a toothbrush to become heavily infected. If you have recurring, minor sore throats try changing your toothbrush about every fortnight.

THUNDER STORMS

Preventing Being Struck By Lightning. When a thunder storm threatens, here are some tips to avoid being struck by lightning.
- Get inside a house, building or metal vehicle that is not a convertible.
- If you cannot reach a building or car do not stand under a tall, isolated tree.
- Do not stand above the surrounding landscape such as on a hill top. Avoid open fields or the beach. Avoid open water if in a small boat.
- Stay away from metal equipment, wire fences, clothes lines, metal pipes and other metal objects that would attract lightning to you.
- If in a forest go to a low area under a thick growth of small trees.

TICKS

Ridding Your Pet Of Ticks.
- Use a cotton wool swab to dab alcohol on the tick. As it reacts by releasing itself from your pet's skin grasp the tick with your thumb and forefinger, twist and yank out.
- If long hair prevents getting at the tick apply margarine or vegetable shortening to the area, then follow the directions above.

TOOTHACHE

What To Do When You Can't Call Your Dentist.
- First, try flossing between teeth in the area of pain. Sometimes, food particles lodged between the teeth can cause discomfort.
- Try cleansing the cavity to remove food debris.
- Apply warm oil of cloves, available at a health food shop. Pour a little in a teaspoon and heat with a match. Dab into the cavity with a toothpick or match.
- For larger cavities mix the oil of cloves with zinc oxide powder to make a thick paste. Press a blob of this mixture into the cavity area with fingertips. Clean off excess with a toothpick.
- Place a well-padded ice bag on the area of pain. Take an aspirin or paracetamol. (Never place aspirin in a cavity. It can cause tooth and tissue damage.)

What To Do If A Crown Comes Off. When a crown comes off and you are unable to get to a dentist, here's what to do. Wash the crown, dry it and put petroleum jelly into it. Then carefully reposition it over your tooth. If you do not do this and the crown is left off for a period of time, it may not be possible for your dentist to re-cement it because the adjacent teeth may have shifted.

Massaging Jaw Muscles. Sometimes a toothache may be caused by tense, sore muscles in your jaw. The pain felt in the mouth mimics a toothache but tense jaw muscles are the real culprit. If this is the cause of your mouth pain, take the index fingers of both hands and gently massage (in a circular motion) the jaw muscles where the jaw connects. Continue this until the pain subsides. If it does not, consult your dentist.

TOOTH DECAY

Cheese To Prevent Tooth Decay. Certain kinds of cheese may help prevent tooth decay, says Dr Charles Schachtele, Professor of Dentistry at the University of Minnesota. Cheeses that work best are Swiss and Cheddar. They prevent acid from forming on teeth and promoting decay.

Avoid Raisins. A study published in the Journal of the American Dental Association says raisins are more harmful to the teeth than any other common snack, including chocolate, biscuits, caramel and fudge. The report says raisins cause more decay because they stick to your teeth.

Toothbrushes And Cavities. It is a good idea to dispose of a toothbrush after about one month. After that bristles become worn and the toothbrush loses its effectiveness and may become contaminated with bacteria. A study in Medical World News reported it takes only 17 to 35 days for a toothbrush to become heavily infected. This is not surprising since a toothbrush provides a warm, moist environment for fast bacterial growth.

Citrus Fruits. Citrus fruits such as lemons, oranges, grapefruit and tangerines contain citric acid which can cause damage to the enamel of your teeth. To avoid damage, rinse your mouth after eating or drinking any citrus fruit. Also avoid the habit of sucking on oranges, grapefruit or lemons.

TRAVEL SICKNESS

Using Ginger Root To Prevent. A recent study showed that two capsules of powdered ginger root, available at health food shops, was twice as effective in stopping travel sickness as 100 mg of Dramamine.

Preventing Travel Sickness In Children. A study published in the New England Journal of Medicine showed that elevating a child in the back seat may prevent travel sickness. When a child is sitting normally in a seat his eyes cannot focus on fast moving objects. He sees only vibrating and bobbing objects. This can cause travel sickness. When a seat is raised he can focus on relatively still objects reducing the effects of the motion.

Other Suggestions.
- Sit where there is the least motion. In a car, that would be in the front seat looking straight ahead. In an aircraft, select a seat over the wing. On a ship, stay in the middle section on deck rather than below.
- Lie in a semi-reclined position and keep your head as still as possible.
- Look ahead at the horizon or close your eyes if watching passing scenery makes you ill.
- Focus on something other than the motion. For example, occupying children with colouring books may be better than having them look out of the window.
- When using a product to prevent travel sickness, such as ginger root or Dramamine, take 30 minutes to an hour before travelling. These products generally do not provide relief after the onset of symptoms.

URINARY TRACT (BLADDER) INFECTIONS

How To Avoid. About a third of all women aged 20 to 40 are likely to suffer from recurring urinary tract infections, says Dr Rosemary Lindan of Western Reserve University. Women get urinary tract infections 10 times as often as men. Here are some tips to avoid this discomfort.

- Drink plenty of water - from six to twelve glasses a day. This will encourage frequent urination which empties the bladder and flushes out bacteria. Diluting the urine also eases urinary symptoms.
- Wipe from front to back after urinating. This will prevent moving faecal bacteria closer to the opening of the bladder. When possible clean the anal and vaginal areas with a stream of water after going to the bathroom.
- Be sure the genital area is clean before sex. Use a spermicidal germicidal lubricant during sex.
- Urinate as soon as possible after sexual intercourse to flush out bacteria. It may be necessary to drink a glass of water before sex so it's possible to

urinate afterwards. This will flush out any bacteria that may have entered the bladder during sex.

- Use a water-soluble lubricant, such as petroleum jelly, if the vagina is dry. If delicate tissues are bruised they may become infected.
- Check with a gynaecologist if a diaphragm may be contributing to your urinary tract infections. If so, another type of contraceptive should be used. A study in the New England Journal of Medicine showed that women who use a diaphragm have twice as many bladder infections as other women.
- Use tampons instead of sanitary towels. Bacteria can more easily build up on towels.
- Take showers instead of baths. Bacteria can easily travel up the urinary tract while you are sitting in the bath.
- Never use bubble bath. It's irritating and can make you more prone to an infection.
- Avoid wearing tight trousers or jeans. Tight clothing contributes to urinary tract bacteria growth.
- Wear cotton pants. They are more absorbent than nylon or synthetic underwear.
- Consider whether symptoms occur after use of spermicidal creams, swimming in a chlorinated pool or cycling.

Cranberry Juice Kills Bacteria. Cranberry juice is sometimes prescribed for bladder infections. Cranberry juice has a high concentration of vitamin C. Just one cup has over 100 mg of the vitamin. When vitamin C is in the urine it promotes health of the bladder, says Dr Alan Gaby of Baltimore, Maryland. Vitamin C can help kill the Escherichia Coli - the most common cause of urinary tract infections.

Cranberry juice also contains hippuric acid which tends to inhibit the growth of bacteria. Another doctor recommends a 6 oz glass of cranberry juice twice a day for bladder infections.

VITAMIN OVERDOSE

More Is Not Always Better. In fact, taking too much of some vitamins can cause health problems over time. This is because some fat-soluble vitamins accumulate in your body and are not eliminated. In the longer term this accumulation can cause you problems.

Vitamin A. Vitamin A can produce toxic symptoms when 5 to 8 times the recommended daily allowance (RDA) is consumed for a long period of time. The RDA for vitamin A is 5,000 IUs. The toxic symptoms may include headache, blurred vision, impaired eyesight and flaking of the skin. It's a good idea to get vitamin A from beta-carotene supplements. With beta-carotene the body absorbs only the vitamin A that is needed.

Vitamin D. Taking too much vitamin D over time can cause weakness, loss of appetite, nausea, body aches and stiffness. Overdose of vitamin D increases absorption of calcium. This excess calcium may be deposited in the heart, lungs, kidneys and even the brain. These calcium deposits can cause organ damage.

Vitamin B-6. Taking daily supplements of vitamin B-6 of 200 mg for over a month can cause convulsions.

Vitamin B-1. Megadoses of vitamin B-1 can cause bad breath.

WARTS

Safe Wart Remover. According to a panel of medical experts working for the US Food and Drug Administration (FDA), only one over-the-counter ingredient is both safe and effective in removing warts. That ingredient is salicylic acid, available in many pharmaceutical preparations. Salicylic acid gets rid of the wart by destroying the outer surface so it can be peeled away. FDA officials warn not to use salicylic acid in the following cases:

- If you are a diabetic or have poor circulation.
- On warts that have hair growing out of them, genital warts or warts on the face or mucous membranes.
- On moles or birthmarks.
- If excessive irritation occurs.
- Near the eyes.

Vitamin E For Warts. Many people report that applying a cream of 28,000 IUs of vitamin E to a wart, once or twice a day, helps get rid of them. Also take 400 IUs of vitamin E daily.

WINE

May Help You Relax. A glass of wine before or after dinner can often help you relax, say medical experts. Inexpensive wines can be just as good as expensive ones. For example, in a test of 160 wines and champagnes judges found it was hard to differentiate the inexpensive wines from the expensive ones. Experts say that a £5 bottle of Californian wine was judged better than a French rosé costing £15. A £3 bottle of Spanish wine was judged as good as a French wine costing £30.

WORKING WOMEN

Have Unhappier Marriages. Wives who have jobs are much less satisfied with their marriages than housewives, says Dr Harold Voth, Professor at the University of Kansas. Working wives have more complaints about their mates and tend to respect them less. They often resent their pay cheques going for household necessities. They would rather spend their earnings on something else.

WRINKLES

Egg Whites. Try an egg white face mask to make your skin smoother. Egg white is made of water and albumin proteins. It nourishes your skin because the water evaporates and the proteins dry on. When you wash off the hardened mask, it removes loose, dead cells, making the skin look smoother and healthier.

SUGGESTED BODY WEIGHTS

Range of Acceptable Weights

Height	Men	Women
(feet-inches)	(pounds)	(pounds)
4'10"		92-119
4'11"		94-122
5'0"		96-125
5'1"		99-128
5'2"	112-141	102-131
5'3"	115-144	105-134
5'4"	118-148	108-138
5'5"	121-152	111-142
5'6"	124-156	114-146
5'7"	128-161	118-150
5'8"	132-166	122-154
5'9"	136-170	126-158
5'10"	140-174	130-163
5'11"	144-179	134-168
6'0"	148-184	138-173
6'1"	152-189	
6'2"	156-194	
6'3"	160-199	
6'4"	164-204	

NOTE: Height without shoes; weight without clothes.

CALORIE CONTENT OF EVERYDAY FOODS

Drinks	**Calories**
Apple juice, canned, half cup	60
Orange juice, fresh, half cup	55
Pineapple juice, canned, unsweetened, half cup	70
Cola-type, 8 oz glass	95
Beer, 3.6% alcohol, 8 oz glass	100
Whisky, gin, rum, vodka, 1.5 oz glass	
80% proof	95
90% proof	110
Table wine, 3.5 oz glass	85

Bread

White, soft crumb, 1 slice	70
White, firm crumb, 1 slice	65
Whole wheat, soft crumb, 1 slice	65
Whole wheat, firm crumb, 1 slice	60

Sweets

Caramels, (1 oz) 3 medium	115
Chocolate creams, 35 to 1 lb, 2 to 3 pieces (1 oz)	125
Chocolate, milk, sweetened, 1 oz	145
Chocolate mints, 20 to 1 lb, 1 to 2 mints (1 oz)	115

Desserts

Apple pie, eighth of 9-inch pie	300
Custard tart, eighth of 9-inch tart	250
Lemon meringue, eighth of 9-inch pie	270
Bread pudding, with raisins, half cup	250
Ice cream, plain	
regular (about 10% fat) half cup	130
rich (about 16% fat) half cup	165

Beef

Corned beef, tinned, 3 oz	185
Hamburger, grilled, sautéed	
regular, 3 oz	245
lean, 3 oz	185
Oven roast, cooked without bone	
cuts relatively fat, such as rib, lean and fat, 3 oz	375
lean only, 3 oz	205
Steak, sirloin, grilled, without bone, lean and fat, 3 oz	330
lean only, 3 oz	175

Lamb

Loin chop, grilled, without bone, lean and fat, 3 oz	305
lean only, 3 oz	160
Leg, roasted, without bone, lean and fat, 3 oz	235
lean only, 3 oz	160

Pork

Bacon, grilled or fried, crisp, 2 thin slices	60

Chop, grilled without bone, lean and fat, 3 oz	335
lean only, 3 oz	230
Ham, cured, cooked without bone, lean and fat, 3 oz	245
lean only, 3 oz	160
Roast, loin, cooked without bone, lean and fat, 3 oz	310
lean only, 3 oz	215

Poultry

Chicken, roasted (no skin), half breast	140
fried (no skin), half breast	160
drumstick, one	80
Chicken pie, home-made, quarter of 9-inch	410
Turkey, roasted, (no skin), light meat, 3 oz	135
dark meat, 3 oz	160

Fish

Haddock, breaded, fried, 3 oz	140
Salmon, grilled or baked, 3 oz	155
tinned, pink, with liquid, 3 oz	120
Sardines, tinned in oil, drained, 3 oz	170
Tunafish, tinned in oil, drained, 3 oz	170

Eggs

Fried in fat, large, one	95
Hard or soft boiled, large, one	80
Omelette, plain, one large egg, milk and fat for cooking	110
Poached, large, one	80
Scrambled in fat, one large egg and milk	110

Vegetables (cooked)

Asparagus spears, 6 medium	20
Broccoli, chopped, half cup	25
Cabbage, half cup	15
Carrots, half cup	25
Cauliflower florets, half cup	15
Corn on the cob, one 5-inch ear	70
Peas, half cup	65
Potatoes, baked, size $2^1/_3$ x $4^3/_4$ inches, one	145
boiled, $2^1/_2$-inch diameter, one	90
chips, home-made, ten $1^1/_2$ x $1/_4$-inch pieces	215
mashed, milk added, half cup	70

Fruits (raw, average size)

Apple	80
Banana	85
Cantaloupe melon, half	80
Grapefruit, half	45
Honeydew melon, 2 x 7-inch wedge	50
Orange	65
Peach	40
Pear	100
Pineapple, diced, half cup	40

Table Of Contents

172

180